S. HRG. 108–404

THE HIDDEN GULAG: PUTTING HUMAN RIGHTS ON THE NORTH KOREA POLICY AGENDA

HEARING

BEFORE THE

SUBCOMMITTEE ON EAST ASIAN AND PACIFIC AFFAIRS

OF THE

COMMITTEE ON FOREIGN RELATIONS UNITED STATES SENATE

ONE HUNDRED EIGHTH CONGRESS

FIRST SESSION

NOVEMBER 4, 2003

Printed for the use of the Committee on Foreign Relations

Available via the World Wide Web: http://www.access.gpo.gov/congress/senate

U.S. GOVERNMENT PRINTING OFFICE

92–834 PDF   WASHINGTON : 2003

For sale by the Superintendent of Documents, U.S. Government Printing Office
Internet: bookstore.gpo.gov   Phone: toll free (866) 512–1800; DC area (202) 512–1800
Fax: (202) 512–2250   Mail: Stop SSOP, Washington, DC 20402–0001

CONTENTS

THE HIDDEN GULAG:
PUTTING HUMAN RIGHTS ON THE NORTH KOREA POLICY AGENDA

TUESDAY, NOVEMBER 4, 2003

U.S. SENATE,
SUBCOMMITTEE ON EAST ASIAN
AND PACIFIC AFFAIRS,
COMMITTEE ON FOREIGN RELATIONS,
Washington, DC.

The subcommittee met, pursuant to notice, at 2:35 p.m. in room SD–419, Dirksen Senate Office Building, Hon. Sam Brownback (chairman of the subcommittee), presiding.

Senator BROWNBACK. Good afternoon. The hearing will come to order.

Hopefully, this hearing will begin to expose the true nature of the North Korean regime and its reputation as one of the worst violators of human rights in the world today.

We'll hear testimony from the author of the recently released report, "The Hidden Gulags: Exposing North Korea's Prison Camps." This was sponsored by the U.S. Committee on Human Rights in North Korea. We'll also see recently smuggled video footage of a labor camp in North Korea for minor offenders. I want to note, too, this is for minor offenders, the footage that we will see. Other witnesses will speak about the need for putting human rights on the agenda in any future dealings with North Korea, and speak more generally about various policy options.

Before we get to the witnesses, I'd like to make some brief comments. First, promoting democracy and freedom in North Korea and ending its nuclear threat do not need to involve military action by the United States. We should explore every possible avenue for a peaceful and democratic resolution of the stalemate on the Korean Peninsula.

How we can peacefully achieve a democratic Korea is one of the issues we will explore at this hearing today. And let me be clear about one thing. A resolution will not be on terms dictated by Kim Jong Il's regime.

We should recall the way Ronald Reagan dealt with the Soviet Union in the 1980s. He called it for what it was, a brutal regime that repeatedly violated the rights of its citizens. He continued to deal with the Soviets out of necessity, but he never forgot, for one moment, the horrors of that regime and the violations of human rights occurring within its borders. He never forgot about the people of that country yearning for freedom and for democracy, and neither should we.

Ronald Reagan did this, however, not as some flag-waving rally for human rights and democracy, but because he knew that profound historic changes were going to happen, not only in the Soviet Union, but in other parts of Europe, as well. He saw the signs of systems failure, and he understood that when people are not free to make their own decisions, a ruler's hold on power is tenuous.

In North Korea, we are seeing similar signs of systems failures. The regime is already collapsing. Free countries should not prop it up, but rather hasten its demise to the totalitarian junk-heap of history.

Here are some of the signs of systems failures in North Korea. China has dispatched 150,000 troops to the border with North Korea, and they're expected to beef it up to upwards of half a million. This isn't simply a function of trying to cutoff refugees desperately trying to escape and survive the conditions in North Korea. Surely the local state security forces can deal with that. Thousands of North Korean refugees are in hiding in northeast China, looking for every venue of escape. We witnessed a similar exodus in Eastern Europe as those totalitarian states were collapsing.

According to the report by the U.S. Committee on Human Rights in North Korea, hundreds of thousand have died of starvation and oppression, while others continue to languish in their gulags. We saw that in Eastern Europe and the Soviet Union before its collapse.

As Dr. Eberstadt, of the American Enterprise Institute, testified before this committee and other Senate hearings, North Korea resorts to criminal activities to earn hard currency in order to keep its regime on life support. With sovereignty and diplomatic privileges as its cover, North Korea is essentially a state-run organized criminal enterprise that is engaged in drugs and arms trafficking, counterfeiting, and other activities across the globe. Given these signs, we must have the resolve to deal firmly with North Korea.

In this context, I'm in the process of preparing comprehensive legislation designed to promote freedom and democracy for the millions who languish in North Korea, and to protect the hundreds of thousands of North Korea refugees that have already fled.

Let me make clear what this bill is not about. It's not about continuing to subsidize the North Korean regime so that it can build and maintain more gulags. The American people will not stand for that.

Having said that, if the administration is able to force North Korea to halt its nuclear program, that is certainly a positive step forward. But North Korea will not get one cent from the United States or other supporters of human rights, I hope, unless it also agrees to make significant improvements into its human-rights situation.

There is no obligation for the United States and its allies to keep the regime on life support.

The American people will not tolerate food aid being skimmed by the North Korean regime for its army and the elites. We must be able to verify and monitor the distribution of food in all parts of North Korea.

I'm hopeful that with the support of key Members of the House and Senate, we will be able to introduce the bill before adjournment.

We have a building across from the Capitol here in Washington, DC, called the Holocaust Museum. Thousands of survivors and their families are gathered this week to pay tribute to the proposition that the world will never forget what happened to the Jewish people during World War II.

There is no question in my mind that had Congress held hearings and made the effort to speak the truth about the Nazi regime in 1943, many lives would have been saved.

There is another message that the Holocaust Museum represents. It also stands for the proposition that we will not remain silent in the face of the kind of horrors that are occurring on a daily basis in North Korea. What you're about to see has been going on for 50 years since the end of the Korean conflict. It's about time such behavior comes to an end. Unless we are willing to speak out about the evils of the North Korean regime, we may, in the words of George Santayana, "be condemned to repeat history."

Our first witness, Mr. David Hawk, is a human-rights investigator and advocate. His worked for the United Nations and other organizations include the Khmer Rouge genocide and the Rwanda massacres. Recently, he's consulted for the Landmine Survivors Network on humanitarian assistance projects in Cambodia and Vietnam.

Mr. Hawk, I look forward to your testimony. And at the conclusion of your testimony, we'll have a short video presentation, which was previously shown by Tokyo Broadcasting Service, who owns its copyrights. And we will see that at the end of this testimony.

Mr. Hawk, I'm delighted to have you here today and look forward to your testimony and your explaining the photographs that you have in front of us, as well.

STATEMENT OF DAVID HAWK, HUMAN RIGHTS INVESTIGATOR, U.S. COMMITTEE FOR HUMAN RIGHTS IN NORTH KOREA, WASHINGTON, DC

Mr. HAWK. Senator Brownback, thank you very much for inviting me to testify today about the nature of the North Korean prison camp system.

As you know, North Korean officials continue to adamantly, strenuously deny that they have any political prisoners or any political prison camps. I hope that the report released last week by the U.S. Committee for Human Rights in North Korea will provide the vocabulary, the analysis, and a modicum of evidence that will enable U.N. officials, diplomats, visiting congressional delegations, journalists, and others with the material and information they need to challenge such denials.

Virtually all of the scores of thousands of Koreans imprisoned in the kwan-li-so political penal forced-labor camps are victims of what the U.N. defines as arbitrary detention. None of those so imprisoned have undergone any judicial process or trial. Most of those imprisoned serve lifetime sentences performing slave labor—usually mining or lumber-jacking, timber-cutting, or agricultural production—under terrible conditions. Most of those imprisoned are there by virtue of a system of guilt by association in which not only the perceived political wrongdoer, but members of his or her family, up to three generations, are imprisoned for life at hard labor.

Virtually all of the kwan-li-so inmates—and the former guards believe that the number 200,000 is the minimal figure of the population of the kwan-li-so camps—are political prisoners. Six such political penal labor camps are believed to be operating currently. Eyewitnesses's accounts of four of these prison camps appear in the report, along with satellite photos of these four political prison camps.

The other component of the North Korean gulag is the kyo-hwa-so prison camps, which, like the kwan-li-so, are characterized by very high rates of deaths in detention from combination of below-subsistence-level food rations combined with hard labor under terrible conditions. But the kyo-hwa-so inmates have been through a judicial process and are given fixed-term sentences. And the inmate population of the kyo-hwa-so forced labor prisons and camps is mixed. Some have been convicted of criminal offenses, others are political prisoners. Such kyo-hwa-so inmates were imprisoned for what would not be criminal acts in a non-totalitarian society. Examples included in the report are those North Koreans in prison and condemned to hard, dangerous labor for singing, or being overheard singing, South Korean pop songs, for listening to South Korean radio, or having met South Koreans while they were in China. This report provides descriptions of seven kyo-hwa-so prison camps and a satellite photograph of Kaechon kyo-hwa-so in South Pyongan Province.

You may have heard, previously, testimony from Soon Ok Lee. She was in Kaechon, and a satellite photograph of the prison camp where she was imprisoned appears in the report.

Similarly, the shorter-term jib-kyul-so provincial detention center inmate populations are also mixed. Some detainees are imprisoned for what are essentially misdemeanor-level offenses, but many others are imprisoned solely for having left North Korea to obtain food or money for food in China or having left their village without authorization to seek food in a neighboring area. These provincial detention facilities and the related ro-dong-dan- ryeon-dae labor training centers constitute a separate system of punishment and forced labor for North Koreans who have been forcibly repatriated from China.

Each of these different prison slave-labor camps are characterized by extreme phenomena of repression. Lifetime imprisonment and guilt by association up to three generations in the kwan-li-so, forced abortion and ethnic infanticide in the provincial detention centers along the North Korea/China border. The practice of torture and extremely high rates of deaths in detention from forced labor and below-subsistence-level food rations permeate the system in these camps at all levels.

The base of information, the data base, on which this report was prepared is outlined in the introduction to the report. For some of the prison camps, we have multiple sources, such as the kwan-li-so at Yodok, where there were four former prisoners provide testimony that ranged in years from 1975 up until the late 1990s.

For other of these prison camps, there are limited, even single, sources. For example, Mr. Kim Yong is the only known prisoner from camp number 14 and camp number 18 to have escaped and subsequently obtained asylum in South Korea.

On the other hand, if North Korean authorities want to disprove the claims made by the former prisoners, it would not be difficult to invite appropriate representatives of the United Nations, the ICRC, or responsible NGOs, such as Amnesty International or Human Rights Watch, to visit the sites which are identified and precisely located in the report.

Until such time as onsite verifications are allowed, the refugee testimonies, as are presented in the report, retain their credence and authority.

Since the authorities in North Korea do not allow onsite verification, the U.S. Committee, with the help of the National Resource Defense Council, was able to obtain satellite photographs of seven different prison camps, prisons, and detention centers, whose landmarks have been identified by the former prisoners from these facilities.

Finally, Senator, I'd like to call your attention to some of the recommendations in the report. First, I hope that Congress will encourage the Bush administration to increase their satellite coverage of the North Korean prison camps. These satellite photographs on display at this hearing are taken from the archives of commercial satellite photo companies. But these commercial satellite photo companies do not have satellites revolving over North Korea anywhere near the frequency or power and scope that the U.S. Government does, and it would be extremely helpful if there would be updated information presented to Members of Congress and others with the appropriate security clearances as to development and activities in these camps. We are able to provide coordinates of longitude and latitude up to a hundredth of a degree.

Second, with respect to the situation of North Koreans in China, I hope that the United States will speak to the Chinese about allowing the UNHCR access to North Koreans in China or, pending that step, simply to stop the repatriation of North Koreans until it can be verified that the extreme punishment of repatriated North Koreans has ceased.

I would also hope that the United States, preferably in cooperation with South Korea and Japan, can approach the Chinese about a program of orderly departure, first asylum and third-country resettlement, if that's the only way to empty out the kwan-li-so penal labor colonies.

Third, as a substantial contributor to the World Food Program in Korea, I would hope that the United States could urge the World Food Program to offer food support to the kyo-hwa-so, jib-kyul-so, and ro-dong-dan-ryeon-dae prisons and prisoners, in order to reduce the high number of deaths and detention from malnutrition, starvation, and related diseases.

And, last, regarding the present six-party talks with North Korea, I have no idea if these negotiations can or will succeed, and perhaps they will be limited to security tradeoffs and arrangements. However, if a more comprehensive solution is envisioned or demanded—that is, one that includes foreign aid to, foreign investment in, and normalized economic relations with North Korea, by which they mean opening up the borders of Europe and North America to goods and materials from North Korea—in that situation, I would hope that the humanitarian and human-rights conditions, some of which are detailed in this report, would also be put on the agenda for consideration at the negotiation.

Thank you, Senator.

[The prepared statement of Mr. Hawk follows:]

PREPARED STATEMENT OF DAVID HAWK, HUMAN RIGHTS INVESTIGATOR, U.S. COMMITTEE FOR HUMAN RIGHTS IN NORTH KOREA, WASHINGTON, DC

THE HIDDEN GULAG: EXPOSING NORTH KOREA'S PRISON CAMPS—PRISONER TESTIMONIES AND SATELLITE PHOTOGRAPHS

Senators, thank you very much for inviting me to testify today on the North Korean prison camps system. As you know, North Korean officials continue to adamantly, strenuously deny that they have political prisoners or political prison camps. I hope that my report,[1] released last week by the U.S. Committee for Human Rights in North Korea will provide the vocabulary, the analysis, and the modicum of evidence that will enable UN officials, diplomats, parliamentarian delegations, journalists and others to challenge such denials.

Virtually all of the scores of thousands of Koreans imprisoned in the *kwan-li-so* political penal forced labor camps are victims of what the UN defines as "arbitrary detention." None of those so imprisoned have undergone any judicial process. Most of those imprisoned serve life-time sentences performing slave labor—usually mining, lumberjacking and timber cutting or agricultural production—under terrible conditions. Most of those imprisoned are there by virtue of a system of guilt by association, in which not only the perceived political wrong-doer, but members of his or her family up to three generations are imprisoned at hard labor. Virtually all of the *kwan-li-so* inmates are political prisoners. Six such political penal labor camps are believed to be operating currently. Eyewitness accounts of four of these prison camps appear in the report, along with satellite photos of these four political prison camps.

The other component of the North Korean gulag is *kyo-hwa-so* prison camps, which like the *kwan-li-so* are characterized by very high rates of deaths-in-detention from combinations of below-subsistence food rations coupled with hard labor under brutal conditions. But the *kyo-hwa-so* inmates have been through a judicial process and are given fixed term sentences. And, the inmate population of the *kyo-hwa-so* forced labor prisons and prison camps is mixed: some have been convicted of criminal offenses: others are political prisoners. Such *kyo-hwa-so* inmates were imprisoned for what would not be criminal acts in non-totalitarian societies. Examples included in this report are those North Koreans imprisoned and condemned to hard, dangerous labor under extremely harsh conditions for singing South Korean songs, listening to South Korean radio, or having met South Koreans in China. The report provides descriptions of seven *kyo-hwa-so* and a satellite photograph of Kaechon, South Pyong-an Province.

Similarly, the shorter-term *jib-kyul-so* provincial detention center inmate populations are also mixed. Some detainees are imprisoned for essentially misdemeanor level offenses. But many others are imprisoned solely for having left North Korea to obtain food or money for food in China. Or having left their village without authorization to seek food in a neighboring area. These provincial detention facilities and the related *ro-dong-dan-ryeon-dae* labor training camps constitute a separate system of punishment and forced labor for North Koreans forcibly repatriated from China.

Each of these different prison-slave labor camps, prisons and detention facilities are characterized by extreme phenomena of repression: life-time imprisonment and guilt by association, up to three generations in the *kwan-li-so;* forced abortion and ethnic infanticide in the provincial detention centers along the North Korea-Chinese border; the practice of torture and extremely high rates of deaths-in-detention from combinations of forced labor and below subsistence food rations permeate the prison and camps system at all levels.

---

[1] The entire report may be accessed at www.hrng.org

The base of information on which this report was prepared is outlined in the introduction. Still, for some of these prison camps we have limited sources, even single sources. For example, Mr. Kim Yong is the only known escapee from Camps 14 and 18 in province known to have obtained asylum. On the other hand, if North Korean authorities want to disprove the claims made by former prisoners, it would not be difficult to invite appropriate representatives of the UN, the ICRC, or responsible NGOs such as Amnesty International or Human Rights Watch to visit the sites identified and located in this report. Until such time as on-site verifications are allowed, the refugee testimonies, such as presented in this report retain their credence and authority. Since the North Korean authorities do not allow on-site verification, the U.S. Committee, with the help of the National Resource Defense Council, was able to obtain satellite photographs of seven different prison camps, prisons and detention centers, whose landmarks have been identified by the former prisoners from these facilities.

Finally, may I call your attention to some of the recommendations of the report.

First, I hope Congress will be able to encourage the Bush Administration to increase their satellite coverage of the NK prison camps.

Second, with respect to the situation of North Koreans in China, I hope that the U.S. will speak to the Chinese about allowing the UNHCR access to North Koreans in China, or pending that step, to simply stop the repatriation of North Koreans until it can be verified that the extreme punishments of repatriated North Koreans has ceased. I would also hope that the United States, preferably in cooperation with South Korea and Japan can approach the Chinese about a program of orderly departure, first asylum and third country re-settlement if that is the only way to empty out the North Korean *kwan-li-so.*

Third, as a substantial contributor to the World Food Program in Korea, I would hope that the United States could urge the WFP to offer food support to the *kyohwa-so, jib-kyul-so* and *ro-dong-dan-ryeon-dae* prisons and prisoners in order to reduce the number of deaths in detention from malnutrition and related diseases.

Fourth, regarding the present six-party talks with North Korea, I have no idea if these negotiations can or will succeed. Or, perhaps they will be limited to security trade-offs and arrangements. However, if a more comprehensive solution is envisioned or demanded—that is one that includes foreign aid to, foreign investment in, and "normalized" economic relations (opening up the borders of Europe and North America for North Korean-produced goods and materials), then I would hope that humanitarian and human rights consideration would also be put on the agenda for consideration.

Senator BROWNBACK. Thank you, Mr. Hawk.

I have looked over your report,[2] a summary of it, and it's, you know, quite clear and explicit, and quite condemning, what's taking place in North Korea.

I wonder, would you give me a couple of minutes and come around and point to these various pictures, and hold them up and say, "Here is what's in this one"? I didn't ask you to do that ahead of time, but you've got a number of these satellite pictures, and these are all from commercial entities, as I understand, from what you said. And just go around and spend a moment, if you could, on each of them, identifying them.

Mr. HAWK. This is a commercial satellite photograph of the entire Korean Peninsula with the selected prison-camp locations of the former prisoners who were interviewed in the report. There are many additional prison camps. These are only the prison camps for which we had former prisoners or guards who I was able to interview who could identify the locations of the camps and their locations are put in this satellite photo by the coordinates of longitude and latitude, so they're quite accurate placements.

This is a partial interview of the kwan-li-so political penal labor colony called Yodok, and, as you can see, this is primarily, an agri-

---

[2]The report, including the satellite photos discussed during Mr. Hawk's testimony, can be found on the U.S. Committee for Human Rights in North Korea's Web site at: www.hrnk.org

cultural prison labor farm in which various crops are grown in the valleys in between the mountain areas.

This is where a fellow by the name of Kang Chul-Hwan was imprisoned from the age of 9 to 19 because of the perceived political mistake his grandfather made.

But you get a sense of the sprawling nature of these prison camps. They're 40 miles long by 20 miles wide, so they're huge areas that are cordoned off and guarded, and you have some sections that are for political prisoners, and then you have other sections isolated from the political prisoners for the families of the political prisoners.

In the report, for each of these red boxes there is a detail of the photograph with the identifications of various places. The prisoners were able to find where they were living, their dormitories, their prison housing units. They were able to find their work sites, and they were able to find the offices of the prison camp and execution and punishment sites in the photographs.

This is a partial overview of both camp number 14, which is on this side of the Taedong River, and camp number 18, which is on this side of the Taedong River. Camp 14 is for perceived political wrongdoers, political prisoners; 18 is for the families of the people over here. This is a coal mine. Camps 14 and 18 are described in the report. This is where Kim Yong, who's currently actually studying theology in Los Angeles, escaped from. He was able, in a close-up, to identify the coal mine where he worked, over here, and he was transferred over here, and he worked on a coal trolley. In the detailed shots you can see the tracks for the coal that was produced here—was shipped to a local power plant about 20 kilometers away. He escaped by hiding in a coal trolley. His job had been to repair the coal trolleys. He jumped into one, and that is how he escaped the camp.

And then you have various details of the camp with the various sections of the prisoners. This is the entrance to the coal mine, where Kim Yong did prison labor for 3 years as a coal miner.

This one has—in another section of the camp, this has his house. He was able to identify the prison dorm where he was held.

In the one over here, which is another detail of camp 14—has in it down here the prison execution site, where they have public executions and hangings for people who violated the prison camp rules, or else were caught trying to escape. And, reasonably enough, the execution site is right near the firing range where the guards practice their rifle shooting.

And then this photograph which I referred to earlier is the kyo-hwa-so, where Soon Ok Lee was imprisoned along with and another woman Ms. Ji, was interviewed for the report, who was arrested because she was overheard singing a South Korean pop song. This is one of the camps.

It's really like a large penitentiary, and the core of which is a textile factory and a shoe factory where the women—this is a place for women prisoners, mixed criminals and politicals, produce shoes and also textiles for export. When Soon Ok Lee was there, they were exporting to Japan, to France, and to Russia the various textile products made by prison slave labor at the Kaechon kyo-hwa-so. But if you look closely, you can see the wall that surrounds the perimeter, just as she describes in her book, and you can see the guard towers along the walls, and various places for supplies and for the factories for shoes and for the guards.

And there are also provincial and sub-provincial detention centers where the repatriated North Koreans are sent. Several of the former inmates drew little sketches that identified the places in the adjacent or interior clinics where the forced abortions took place or where the birthing rooms where, where babies were suffocated. And several months after we had those sketches, we were able to get the satellite photographs of the town, and the women and the men from these jib-kyul-so were able to find, in a large satellite photograph of the town, after several magnifications they could find the buildings and the small detention facilities. You can see that they correspond to the sketches, so you can see the birthing rooms, and you can also see the storage rooms where, according to the testimony of the foreign prisoners, the suffocated fetuses were kept prior to burial.

Senator BROWNBACK. Thank you very much. Thank you,

Mr. HAWK. That's very graphic and specific.

We will now have the video presentation, and I believe, rather than Mr. Hawk, Pastor Shin was going to narrate us through this video presentation.

Pastor Shin, if you could come forward—he has worked a great deal on human rights in this. And I would note to people that this is previously shown by Tokyo Broadcasting Service. They own the copyrights to this. This is, I am told, of a misdemeanor camp, so this would be the most minor-of-offenses type of prison camp.

And let's go ahead and start with that. And, Mr. Douglas Shin, as you see fit to jump in here and to explain, please do so.

Mr. SHIN. Before we start the video, I'd like to make some comments. As Mr. Hawk has explained, there are three tiers in the North Korean penal system. The lowest level is the kyo-hwa-so or labor training camps, the image of which we are about to see. Kyo-hwa so is, by the way, the Russian word for labor training camp. Kyo-hwa-so is only for the smallest of crimes, usually misdemeanors. Sentencing is usually up to 1 year. There are over 200 of these kyo-hwa-sos, one in each county of North Korea. At great risk to himself, the videographer who has taken these images has provided the first-ever video of a labor training camp of North Korea.

These images were first aired in Tokyo on TBS and, as I understand it, was also shown by Reuters. My understanding is that these videos were not shown in South Korea, although there were press reports about them. This would be the first time that these videos are being shown in the United States.

As I understand it from my sources, all the video clips are from a labor training camp in ro-dong-dan-ryeon-dae, which is the official term for labor training camp. This is the northernmost province of North Korea, right on the Chinese border.

So we'd like to start with the first clip. The people you see sitting on the left are very likely former refugees who have been forcefully returned from China. Ordinary refugees who have left China and are rounded up and sent back to North Korea are sentenced to the equivalent of a misdemeanor, and they're sent to a kyo-hwa-so, like this.

If a former refugee is determined to have dealt with missionaries in China or even tried to flee to South Korea or elsewhere, the sentence is 7 years to life in either a penitentiary that is kyo-hwa-so or a political prisoners camp that is kwan-li-so.

And second clip, please.

They're saying, "giddy-up, giddy-up" in Korean. This is a video of workers moving a train car, presumably after having loaded it. Inmates are forced to move the train car, as there is no fuel to start the engine and work it. Please notice that there are women pushing the car, as well.

And the third one, please.

OK, here you see workers removing wood and building a new roof within the camp grounds. See the truss structure that is not quite completed yet. There's a soldier right in the middle ground. OK, please note women and children are also working in this camp.

And the fourth one.

This is simply a video of detainees lined up, probably for a meal, because they don't have tools at hand.

The narration goes "kyo-hwa-so inmates," kind of whispering to the camera.

And the final and fifth one, please.

Here you see inmates lined up to march. Yes, here you see inmates lined up to march, with tools in hand. They are most likely finishing a job and heading back to the dormitory. The first part of the conversation goes, "They've got to be inmates." And the other interlocutor, probably standing next to the videographer, goes, "Yeah, they have to be. They ought to be on their way to the dormitory at the end of the day."

OK, thank you very much.

Senator BROWNBACK. Thank you very much, Mr. Douglas Shin, for sharing those with us in the first-ever, as I understand it, showing of those in the United States, these clips of a misdemeanor labor camp.

I ask now that Ambassador Palmer and Professor Mochizuki join Mr. Hawk at the table. In the interest of time, I'd like to ask everyone, if they could, to summarize their comments.

Ambassador Palmer has served in policy positions at the State Department in the Nixon, Ford, Carter, Reagan, and first Bush administrations, including launching the National Endowment for Democracy. He organized and participated in the first Reagan/Gorbachev summit as the State Department's top criminologist. And as the U.S. Ambassador to Hungary, he helped persuade its last dictator to leave power. Ambassador Palmer is the author of a fabulous new book that I'll put a plug in for here, "Breaking the Real Axis of Evil."

Ambassador Palmer, delighted to have you here.

Mike Mochizuki is professor of Political Science and International Affairs at George Washington University—I hope I got somewhere close to the correct pronunciation.

Together with his colleague at the Brookings Institute, Michael O'Hanlon, Professor Mochizuki is the coauthor of "The Crisis on the Korean Peninsula: How to Deal with a Nuclear North Korea."

Mr. O'Hanlon was to testify today, but he had a scheduling conflict and could not join us.

Ambassador Palmer, you're certainly no stranger to these neighborhoods. I look forward to your testimony and the floor is yours.

STATEMENT OF HON. MARK PALMER, PRESIDENT, CAPITAL DEVELOPMENT CORPORATION, WASHINGTON, DC

Ambassador PALMER. Yes, good. Thank you, Mr. Chairman. It's a pleasure to be with you today.

I think it's very important that we be clear, right off, about what the goal is. The goal is to help the North Korean people liberate themselves from this gulag, both the gulag that we've seen and the larger gulag which is North Korea, to achieve democracy, and to unite peacefully with their fellow Koreans in the South. In my judgment, this will require the ouster of the dictator, Kim Jong Il, and we need a comprehensive strategy to achieve that goal.

In 1972, Brezhnev demanded the same thing that Kim Jong Il has just demanded—that is, a nonaggression pact and trade and economic assistance—and President Nixon responded in that year by saying, "Fine, I'll negotiate about those two things, but you have to add a third basket—human rights, freedom of contact, freedom of travel. You have to have a human-rights basket." And, of course, as we all know, that was the Helsinki process, and it ended up in encouraging a tremendous expansion of freedom in Eastern Europe and ultimately in bringing down the Communist regimes. I think it would be reasonable for all of us to ask President Bush to repeat that lesson. That is to say that we are willing to talk with Kim Jong Il about his desiderata, but we're going to demand that he add the third basket, and we repeat the Helsinki process.

This is important, because the only reason that a dictator can remain in power is if people, the people of his nation, cooperate—passively, out of fear, or for whatever other reason, they cooperate. And the whole game, in my judgment—having lived in and studied a lot of these regimes, the whole game is to get the people to noncooperate, to get to the point where they say, enough is enough. And we, in the free world, have an obligation to help them get to that point.

Now, how to do that? First, I think it's terribly important to recognize that we must communicate with the people of North Korea, we must open up the country, we must let them know that they're not alone, and we must help them believe that they can, in fact, join South Korea and become a normal country. An invaluable avenue for that, of course, is media penetration. It's really a disgrace that Dr. Norbert Vollertsen does not get more support in getting radios into North Korea. Having radios capable of receiving Radio Free Asia and South Korean stations is really of tremendous importance. All of us who lived in Eastern Europe during the period when Communists were brought down know that radio broadcasting, and now television and the Internet, are really central to the process. Members of the elite in North Korea have greater access to information, and we need to work on them, as well, through these same channels.

There is also, of course, a Korean diaspora, including a sizable Korean community in Japan, and I think that we need to work hard on turning some of those people, on gaining agents of influence from within that community, many of whom, of course, are sympathetic, or have been historically sympathetic, to the North Korean Communist regime. I think there is an opportunity there to penetrate the North through that community.

Exchanges have worked very well in opening up and ultimately bringing down Communist regimes, and I am a strong proponent of more exchanges with North Korea, even if in the beginning they're timid and not exactly what we want.

I, for example, started the first business school, the first MBA program in a Communist country, and I think that things like that, even through they're not explicitly political, can make a difference, and we may have to start at that end of the spectrum.

I don't think we're going to get a lot of cooperation out of China. My own sense is that because they are a dictator, that mostly they're supporting Kim Jong Il. And although I agree we should put pressure on them to cooperate on the refugees, my own sense of the bottom line is that they're really on the wrong side and are likely to continue to be on the wrong side.

Russia's another situation. It's, sort of, a half democracy or half dictatorship. I think with Putin there is a chance, and we should work hard on him, to let refugees come out into Russia and to create the kind of flows that we saw, and I personally saw, coming through Hungary in 1989, which really is what led to the collapse of East Germany.

It's very, very important that we begin to talk about reunification in very concrete ways. I was particularly pleased to see that in the paper he submitted, Mr. Hwong, the most senior defector from North Korea, talked about four stages. I think it's really important, in shifting a lead opinion in South Korean to the point where they're willing to really encourage change in North Korea, encourage the fall of the Communists. It's important to reassure them that this can be done in a stable way, in a way that's not going to overwhelm the South Korean economy.

So I think it's very important to begin now to do detailed planning and, most importantly, to publicize that detailed planning on radio and television and the Internet to the North. It can be done in a stable way. I participated personally in doing it in Eastern Germany, where I was a large-scale investor, and I think there are some lessons to learn from that experience in Eastern Germany, some things not to do, as well as things to do.

But I think the most important thing is to begin the process, and do it very publicly, so that all governments—Japan, Korea, ourselves—really will get enthusiastic about bringing down the regime and not be hesitant the way we are today.

At the end of the day, the only thing that really works well is people-power, in my judgment. If we look at all of the change that has taken place, not only in Communist regimes, but in the Philippines, in Indonesia and Argentina and Chile, and, in fact, in South Korea, itself, in ousting dictators, what really works is getting a nonviolent people's movement going, first in the underground, first through covert literature, covert printing presses, and ultimately above-ground, taking control of the whole state through strikes, general strikes, boycotts, and the 198 different techniques, which are outlined in Gene Sharp's very good book, "From Dictatorship to Democracy." There are 198 different techniques that have been used for achieving justice through nonviolent means, and we, on the whole, I think, don't understand this world. We are accustomed to thinking that either we do it through broad-scale sanctions, economic sanctions, or we do it through military means, or we do it through hope. All those things, in my judgment, are much less important than learning the lessons of Solidarity. How did Solidarity get organized in the underground? How did they actually do it? How did it happen in these other countries? We can learn those lessons. My book—thank you for mentioning—goes on at great length about how to do this. That is, how to help the North Koreans get organized over the coming months and years, and eventually push this terrible tyrant out of office.

In my prepared testimony, Mr. Chairman, I go on about this at some length. I won't take the time to do it now.

But let me just say that I think the main thing is a hangup for most people is that they look at the regime in Pyongyang, and they say, this is a brutal regime, and it's not going to tolerate nonviolent resistance. It's just going to kill everybody or put them in these camps. That's a reasonable question, but the answer is that people in very, very brutal situations have succeeded with nonviolent revolt, have succeeded in paralyzing countries and bringing down dictators again and again and again. Even in the heart of Berlin in the middle of the Second World War, a group of women went out and struck and did a sit-in and got their Jewish husbands released from Auschwitz. And Hitler was certainly not faint of heart. He was not a man unwilling to use force against peaceful demonstrators. But it worked in Berlin in 1943. In my judgment, it can work in Pyongyang today. But we need to get organized and to support it.

It is really striking to me that, if you look at my former employer, the State Department, or any other part of the U.S. Government, including the CIA, there is no one, no part of the bureaucracy that's committed to organizing nonviolent resistance movements. No one. There's no one with any expertise, there's no one who gets up in the morning and says, OK, I'm going to work with the 43 different countries that are under dictators, I'm going to work with the people of that country to organize these kind of movements, and we're going to do this peacefully, but we're going to do it. We're not set up for that, and that's really a disgrace. It's the biggest single weakness in our national-security apparatus, in my judgment.

I think outsiders can do a huge amount to de-legitimize Kim Jong Il. And, as I said before, that is the name of the game. We need to show that "the emperor has no clothes."

One of the ways to do that would be to do what is now increasingly being done under international practice, and that is to indict him, to set up an international tribunal to go through all of the elements of criminality, which, as you said earlier, Mr. Chairman, he is guilty of. You mentioned drugs, you mentioned supply of weapons to other rogue regimes. In addition to that, I would add the fact that his behavior led directly to the starvation death of two million people. Clearly that is a crime against humanity. He is implicated in the assassination of South Korean cabinet ministers in Burma. That is murder. He is implicated in the downing of a civilian Korean airliner in the 1980s. That is terrorism. I mean, you can go down a long list of things that would form the basis for an indictment. And I think David Hawk's magnificent and detailed report is precisely one of the things that could be used in an indictment.

By indicting him, we show that this man, who likes to think of himself as a form of God, that this man is nothing better than a common criminal. I think we need to get on with doing that.

And this is my final suggestion, Mr. Chairman. Another thing that could, in my judgment, really work well is to remember what Prime Minister Churchill and President Roosevelt did with their fireside chats during World War II.

By speaking to the free world emotionally and strongly, they rallied the free world to defeat the fascists and to win the war.

I think that every democratic leader in the world should, on a weekly or monthly basis, broadcast into North Korea—of course, in the Korean language—a message of hope and encouragement, with some lessons of how this has been done in other places, and confidence that they are going to get freedom.

In 1981—you mentioned President Reagan, and, as I think you know, I worked with President Reagan during that period—we got over 20 Prime Ministers and Presidents of democratic countries to tape televised messages to broadcast into Poland, into Solidarity, of exactly this nature. So there is precedent for this, and I think it would have a huge effect in North Korea if they heard the Prime Ministers of Japan and England and Italy and many other countries, including, of course, the President of the United States, speaking to the people of North Korea and saying, we are on your side. You are going to achieve your freedom, and here's how to do it.

Thank you, Mr. Chairman.

[The prepared statement of Ambassador Palmer follows:]

PREPARED STATEMENT OF AMBASSADOR MARK PALMER, PRESIDENT, CAPITAL
DEVELOPMENT CORPORATION, WASHINGTON, DC

Let us be clear about our goal. We want to help the North Korean people liberate themselves from the gulag, achieve democracy and unite peacefully with their fellow Koreans in the South. This will require the ouster of the dictator, Kim Jong Il. We need a comprehensive strategy to achieve that goal.

In December 2002 Kim Jong Il created a new crisis by admitting that he had been conducting a secret program to develop nuclear weapons, in violation of the 1994 agreement with the United States. He threatened war if the United States did not agree to negotiate a nonaggression pact and restart economic assistance in return for his, again, promising not to develop nuclear weapons. This presents an extraordinary opportunity for the United States and South Korea to move "From Helsinki to Pyongyang"—the title of a statement of principles that Michael Horowitz of the Hudson Institute and I conceived and drafted and for which we secured leading Americans as cosigners. The *Wall Street Journal* published the statement on 17 January, 2003. We argue that just as President Richard Nixon in 1972 agreed to negotiations on Leonid Brezhnev's demands for a nonaggression pact and improved economic cooperation but insisted on broadening the agenda to include human rights, so President Bush should propose to open negotiations on such a Helsinki-like three-basket agenda with North Korea. The animating insight of Helsinki was that, by publicly raising human rights issues to high-priority levels, the United States would set in motion forces that would undermine the legitimacy of the Soviet communist empire, and so it turned out to be. By formally acknowledging in Helsinki the legitimacy of such rights as the free exchange of people, open borders, and family reunification, the communists opened the floodgates of dissent and brought about their eventual ouster.

Would Kim Jong Il agree to enter into such a negotiation and agreement? In 2002 and 2003 he is showing signs of desperation, and searching for new solutions to mounting problems. In 2002, he introduced a modest reform in the setting of wages and prices, quite likely in part the result of his study trips to China and Russia. In his belligerent way, he is literally begging for relations with, and help from the United States. While he is no Gorbachev 1984-1985, there are some similarities—which we should exploit.

Of the 43 remaining Not Free countries, North Korea is the only one that has yet even to take a cautious step into stage one of the three stages of democracy development set forth in my book "Breaking the Real Axis of Evil: How to Oust the World's Last Dictators by 2025." It has no proto-civil society, no legalistic culture to influence, no free media. It is far more isolated than the pre-Helsinki Soviet Bloc. Material privation surpasses that in the 1960s and 1970s Soviet Bloc, which failed its citizens miserably, but made at least some pretense of having a consumer base.

In fact, thanks to the resilience of the human spirit and imagination, countries are rarely as locked down as they seem from without. The people of North Korea can be persuaded that there is light at the end of the tunnel, and that they can rejoin with their relations in the South in a united, democratic, and open Korea. The democracies, especially those with a strong presence in the region like the United States and Japan, in partnership with the Republic of Korea, a charter member of the Community of Democracies, need to make communicating with the people of North Korea their first priority. Once the brutalized people of North Korea begin to believe that they can work to change their destiny, and that they will have all the help the democracies can possibly provide, the rotten edifice will begin to crumble. But there is no time to lose.

An invaluable avenue is media penetration, which is not impossible in North Korea. People have radios even in the countryside. But we need to ensure that they have radios that can receive foreign broadcasts. Dr. Norbert Vollertsen's efforts, along with those of his South Korean colleagues, to send in such radios are a vital part of the larger strategy. Radio Free Asia has a Korean-language service, and South Korean stations can be received. Building up the Radio Free Asia Korean Service from its current four hours a day to a full-time service would take a modest spike in funding, and considering the potential dividends, the resources need to be found. A concerted effort to get through to the North Korean public in this manner is essential, even with the attendant jamming and monitoring.

Members of the elite in North Korea have greater access to information from outside, through satellite television, the Internet, and other media. They must get a consistent message that there is a future for those who are willing to switch their allegiance to the side of the people—and that the regime is doomed in any case owing to its own failings. They must also understand that should the leadership lash out in its self-imposed death throes, the response will be withering and total. The military, security, and foreign affairs elites' access to international media is essential to the regime. By using these conduits, the democracies can work to reduce the chance for a conflagration when the regime crumbles. High-level officials have defected before, some in recent years. There is no doubt they are taking the risk of defection for a reason. Certainly they know how low North Korea's dictators have laid the country, and how backward it is today. Now they must be shown a way out. The intelligence services of the democracies need to recruit agents of influence in this rarefied stratum. If the North Korean army and security forces can be persuaded not to turn on dissidents at home or against "enemies" abroad, and if the North Korean people can be empowered to take the necessary risks, the shift to democracy could follow very quickly.

The democratic world must work within Japan's sizable Korean community to find ways to get inside and funnel information out. While this community contains a great many North Korean agents and still more sympathizers, even this can be turned into an asset. Interrogating and turning North Korean agents, with all the attendant risks, will at the very least give a clearer picture of North Korea's support network. If these resources are squeezed or redirected toward the struggle for democracy, the regime will feel real pressure.

Such exchanges with the outside world as still exist must be exploited. Russia, at least nominally a democracy, continues to court cold-war-era allies. But North Korea cannot be seen as an ally that produces any financial or strategic gain for Moscow. Following the terrorist attacks on the United States, Russia's President, Vladimir Putin, has tried to draw closer to the United States. An opportunity to change tack is now at hand. President Bush should communicate to Putin that he sees a peaceful transition to democracy in North Korea as being in the interests of

16

both the United States and Russia, and that Moscow has an important role to play in assuring a "soft landing." Broadcast facilities in the Russian far east could help increase the radio footprint—and the frequencies used—for reaching the North Korean general population. Russia's border with North Korea, though relatively short, allows for some defections, refugee flows, and interaction with North Korean authorities. Furthermore, a declared policy of offering political asylum to those who escape should be adopted. A sufficient flow of refugees could, as in former East Germany, lead to the collapse of the regime without any bloodshed or war. If Russia wants to be considered a democracy and a partner in the war on terrorism, its actions with regard to North Korea, as well as the post-Soviet "near abroad," rogue states, and its own dirty war in Chechnya, need to be the proof of such a commitment to a common goal.

China, which shares a much longer border with North Korea, has a deeper, more significant relationship with Pyongyang—a relationship among dictatorial regimes that feel besieged by the democratic world's pull. While China is somewhat more open, it is integral to maintaining the regime it saved from annihilation in the Korean War. There is far greater interchange between China and North Korea. Defections and refugees from North Korea are common—some three hundred thousand in the past few years. Consistent with the rest of Chinese human rights practice, some are forcibly returned to North Korea. Others, as is the case with illegal aliens the world over, are kept in essentially chattel-slavery conditions in China. The communist regime's quest for international respectability, though doomed by its own essential nature, could be used to advantage in this most dire circumstance. It is against international law to return refugees to countries where they will likely be tortured or killed. Chinese commitments—indeed exhortations—that international law must be the basis for relations among nations should be invoked. In addition, this is the most permeable border into North Korea, and better intelligence on the state of the regime and the people of North Korea is best gathered here. Democracies should fund the resettlement in South Korea of Koreans who manage to escape the North Korean border guards.

The bottom line is that Beijing needs to be forced to accept that North Korea will eventually reunify with South Korea in a democratic Korean state, and that the democracies wish to manage this, starting the process sooner rather than later. Of course, if China itself is democratized earlier than North Korea this problem evaporates.

In addition to all this external activity, the democracies need to work to get inside the country directly. Why not up the ante by announcing that the United States, and other democracies wish to open embassies in Pyongyang? With the right talent in even a handful of democratic embassies, the influence of democracies in North Korea—and over developments there—would increase exponentially. Like all embassies, these should be freedom houses, with Internet access and facilities where people can safely meet. The ambassadors and all their diplomatic staff need to make themselves visible on the scene in Pyongyang, testing their limits, traveling to the hinterland, reporting and networking and influencing, even passing out free radios able to receive foreign broadcasts, as our embassy office in Cuba has been doing.

Under the leadership of the South Koreans, the democracies and NGOs need to vastly expand educational, cultural, scientific, people-to-people, and other exchanges with North Koreans. This tried-and-true method had huge impact on opening up the USSR and Eastern Europe and can work in North Korea as well. Kim Jong Il has been willing to explore exchanges, although very tentatively and with repeated backsliding. Even if the initial areas the dictator is interested in should be restricted to such subjects as management training, learning how the World Bank and other international development institutions function and how commercial law works, the democracies should see this as the beginning of a process. While nervous and paranoid, Kim Jong Il, like most dictators, may begin to think he is smart enough to avoid the fate of others before him who thought they could control everything. We need to believe that he will fail once enough opening occurs.

Managing the shift to reunification should start now. Because regimes rarely crumble according to a timetable, having a plan in place for the disintegration of the North Korean regime is imperative. The neighborhood needs to buy into the overall plan, or, as with China, be willing to stay out of the way. The whole democratic world must reassure the region, and Seoul most of all, that it will have resolute backup—including resources—when the process gains its own momentum. Fear of being overwhelmed is palpable, and understandable given the massive disparity that has grown between North and South Korea. This fear is perhaps the largest barrier to active South Korean government support for regime change in the North. They need reassurance that the process can be managed. The time to begin planning for what can be done in all conceivable scenarios is now.

A major reason to begin post-communist planning now is to do it publicly, broadcast it to North Korea and therefore help raise expectations there, create momentum, make the prospect of radical change seem real and near-term. No dictatorship can long survive once the people withdraw their cooperation.

Already, South Koreans and others are studying how Germany went about its unification in 1990, and what is to be avoided. While the analogy is imperfect, there are still lessons to learn. One obvious "don't" is not to convert the North Korean currency on a basis too favorable to it. This killed East Germany's one competitive advantage—low labor costs. Labor mobility will also have to wait for some time, until the North's economy has made some advances, so as not to swamp the South with cheaper labor and again, not to deny northern Korea its natural advantage in attracting investment. Squaring this need with the inevitable drive for family reunification and freedom of movement will be a difficult equation, and one that requires serious thinking now. Perhaps Korea should be reunited in principle after the dictator's ouster but with some degree of separation and autonomy for a transition period. A positive lesson from Germany's unification: building up infrastructure pays big dividends in enabling economic growth, attracting domestic and foreign investment, and stemming the exodus to more affluent areas. North Korea was once the country's industrial base, and industry requires serviceable roads, ports, railways, and communications systems.

Cadres of South Korean police, administrators, and other managers will need to move north to help make the transition as smooth as possible. Northerners need to be brought into the process at all stages. Most important will be the early introduction of democratic political institutions and getting to the point where North Koreans can manage local matters in the same way South Koreans already do.

One of the most positive models for a liberated North Korea is the example of South Korea. In a single lifetime, South Korea has risen from being considered a hopeless backwater under dictators to joining the Organization for Economic Cooperation and Development—the club of the world's richest democracies. South Koreans also had to struggle against and overcome dictatorship to achieve their freedom. Their ingenuity and know-how are already on hand.

A campaign to help bring the world's most repressive regime down, with the North Koreans themselves leading the way for their own liberation, can make an entirely free and united Korea a reality. In parallel with all the other steps outlined above, from the outset we must be working with North and South Koreans and others to organize a non-violent movement to achieve this objective. In a sense, all the other steps are designed to open the space for a nonviolent movement to operate and succeed.

Trying to force dictators to modify the worst aspects of their behavior may certainly help to lessen the human suffering they cause. Soviet leader Nikita Sergeyevich Krushchev closed down much of Stalin's gulag; and we should strive to get Kim Jong Il to do the same. But softening repression does not eliminate its cause; eliminating the dictator is the only way to do that. History provides no account of a dictator being converted into a democrat while still in power, or of relinquishing power of his own volition. The only way for democracy to emerge is for the dictator to go.

How the dictator is challenged determines whether and how quickly he can be ousted, and it also has a crucial effect on whether sustainable democracy ensues. Armed rebellions usually fail, often even before they can begin. Even if they succeed, what comes after is typically no better, and frequently worse, than what they displace. Leaders of guerrilla movements are adept at the use of violence and take those skills with them when they take over presidential mansions: that is why violent revolutions typically produce repressive regimes. The people inherit only a new set of jailers.

But there is another set of strategies for dissolving dictatorial power and establishing democracy, and it has a remarkable record of success. In their seminal book, "A Force More Powerful", Peter Ackerman and Jack Du Vall document a dozen cases in which nonviolent popular movements prevailed against seemingly overwhelming odds and took power away from arbitrary rulers. My own experiences in the U.S. civil rights movement and in diplomatic service in communist countries confirm their view that political systems that deny people their rights can best be taken apart from the inside by the people themselves—of course with substantial assistance from outside.

No dictator can hold power without sowing the seeds of popular discontent. Payoffs to cronies and constables who crack down on opponents eventually exude the smell of corruption, which is always deeply unpopular. The mothers and fathers of young dissidents who are "disappeared" do not forget who is responsible for sundering their families. And few dictators are known for their brilliance in economic management: the economic crises that frequently follow can pile up more dry tinder of public resentment.

From the moment when the match of organized nonviolent opposition is first struck to the day that the dictator steps down, years can elapse—or only weeks. Almost a decade passed between the first stirrings of organized dissidence against the Polish communist regime in the early 1970s and the appearance of Solidarity in the midst of the Gdansk shipyard strike. But forty years earlier, a general strike by the citizens of El Salvador had toppled a military tyrant in a matter of days. The difference is not in how much violence the state is prepared to use—the Salvadoran general was one of his country's bloodiest rulers. What makes for success is developing and communicating clear objectives for the struggle, organizing and mobilizing people on a wide scale, applying maximum pressure to the pillars of a regime's support, and protecting the movement from inevitable repression.

In his landmark tract "From Dictatorship to Democracy" which has been translated into a dozen languages and used as a bible by dissidents from Burma to Serbia, Gene Sharp—the master theoretician of nonviolent conflict—identifies 198 separate methods of nonviolent action. From social and economic boycotts to industrial and rent strikes, and from outright civil disobedience to physical interventions such as sit-ins and occupations, the panoply of nonviolent weapons is far more diverse and inventive than the broadcast media's preoccupation with street marches would lead idle viewers to imagine.

That nonviolent resistance can be at once robust and precise, widespread and carefully timed, is typically unexpected by outsiders, but not by the dictators who are its targets. They do not share the common misconceptions that nonviolent action is passive and reactive and that its leaders are amateurs or pacifists. Nonviolent movements that develop a systematic strategy to undermine their opponents and seize power are deliberately engaging in conflict, albeit with different resources and weapons.

Even though these strategies do not use guns or explosives, they are not forms of conflict for the fainthearted. Nonviolent fighters often have to make protracted physical and economic sacrifices before they liberate their peoples. Many have to endure arrest, imprisonment, and torture. Many have been murdered. Yet tens of thousands of them, in conflict after conflict on five continents, have willingly faced these risks, in the interest of achieving freedom or justice.

Shrewd leadership can help them minimize risks and maximize the political damage their movement inflicts on the dictator. In movements that need people at the working level of society to join open or clandestine opposition, leaders can enlarge the ranks only by showing people that the goals of the struggle are worthy, the strategy sound. So unlike organizations that employ violence, nonviolent movements cannot be operated like an army, strictly from the top down. Their leaders have to rely on the same skills that are needed in running a democracy: persuading people to go along and encouraging initiative at the grass roots. A nonviolent campaign is effective when it overstretches the capacity of a dictator to maintain business as usual; but it can do that only when it empowers people everywhere to challenge his control.

Nonviolent power is therefore always rooted in the mind and action of the individual, and sometimes that action seems innocuous when the struggle is young. As Jan Bubec, the Czech student leader has said, most of the movements against communist rulers in central and eastern Europe first took the form of samizdat, or self-published books, pamphlets, and other literature. The civic action to curb the military dictatorship in Argentina in the late 1970s began with a handful of unsophisticated mothers of the disappeared marching in the capital's central square. Nonviolent combatants understand something that dictators do not: to be sustainable, social or political action has to be built on the choice of individuals to engage in it, not on state edicts that prod unwilling subjects into compliance.

Although nonviolent resistance begins with the individual citizen, it has far more potential than violent insurrection to enlist all parts of the oppressed society in the cause. While violent skirmishing with police or soldiers may appeal to young firebrands, it frightens off older people and those without a taste for physical confrontation—in other words, the most stable elements of civil society, whose support is essential for lasting social or political change. By giving people from all walks of life (even children) ways of participating in a movement, nonviolent strategies enlarge the inventory of resources and tools available to undermine a regime.

This eclectic, inclusive approach to mobilizing support can even extend to people within the regime. Dissatisfaction with a dictator is not limited to those who are politically motivated to oppose him. From lower-level apparatchiks all the way up to the praetorian guard, there is often fear and ambivalence in the ranks of the dictator's chosen servants and defenders. The greater the repression that the dictator has employed, the greater the opportunity to subvert the loyalty of those defenders—but not if the movement vilifies them. When Ferdinand Marcos fell in the Philippines in 1986, and when Slobodan Milosevic fell in Serbia in 2000, their own military officers and police refused final orders to crack down on the opposition. That could not have happened had nonviolent organizers demonized or picked fights with security and military services.

Whether it is manifested in crowded public rallies or the emptiness of boycotted stores, in the boisterous occupation of key factories or the public stillness of a general strike, the vitality of a nonviolent movement necessarily raises popular expectations that it can work where other methods may have failed. Unless people are encouraged by the chance of victory to take action, they will never believe that change is possible. Nothing aids a dictator like the assumption that he cannot be vigorously challenged and when he is challenged the confidence of those whose support he requires to remain in power begins to erode. Then, when a movement's momentum builds from one engagement to the next, the whole nation will realize that the dictator's survival is in question.

No dictator is exempt from having to face this question once a nonviolent movement opens up space for opposition. If we think that the dictators in Beijing and Pyongyang are too ruthless to be bothered by nonviolent challengers, we should revisit the story of Charlotte Israel, the German woman who organized a sit-in demonstration in the heart of Berlin in World War II and forced the Nazis to release her husband and thousands of other Jewish spouses who had been taken to the death camps.

North Korea definitely offers reasons for optimism. It is perhaps the most brittle dictatorship in the world today. Seldom has a regime more fully failed its people and had as little legitimacy and popular support. We know from senior defectors that even those immediately around Kim Jong Il are more afraid than loyal, and that he himself is intensely afraid of being overthrown.

We need to develop a training and support program for a non-violent movement for and inside North Korea, benefiting from the experience in South Korea, the Philippines, Indonesia, eastern Europe and elsewhere. Leaders from those successful movements should train Koreans. A volunteer cadre of those who have escaped from North Korea could form one core group for training in organization and conflict techniques. But others in South Korea and beyond can play important roles.

Outsiders can help by delegitimizing Kim Jong Il. We need a new class of dictator-ousting sanctions narrowly targeted on him, as opposed to broad economic and other sanctions which wall off North Koreans, punish an already suffering people, reinforce the gulag and Kim's control. One such sanction gaining international precedent is to indict and try a dictator for crimes against humanity in a specially instituted tribunal. The basis for an indictment against Kim Jong Il is clear. David Hawk's magnificent and detailed report provides substantial material. Kim Jong Il also should be indicted for the deaths of some two million Koreans from starvation. He is also implicated in the assassination of South Korean cabinet ministers in Burma and the downing of a Korean airliner in the 1980s. I urge that dictatorship itself be declared a crime against humanity; by definition it denies an entire people of rights guaranteed under a host of international agreements adhered to even by North Korea. By treating Kim Jong Il as the criminal he is, we will undermine his attempt to appear almost like a god. We will show that the emperor has no clothes. This is profoundly important in building the will to resist and oust him.

Outsiders also could help instill the will to resist among North Koreans by the sort of fireside chats which Prime Minister Churchill and President Roosevelt used to give the free world the courage to resist and defeat the fascists in World War II. Democratic leaders should make a weekly or monthly practice of speaking to the North Korean people via radio, television and the Internet. We persuaded over twenty prime ministers and presidents of democracies to join in broadcasting to Poland and Solidarity in the 1980s.

Let us finish the job of bringing democracy to the Korean peninsula through the diplomacy of opening and liberation, and inspiring and supporting people power.

Senator BROWNBACK. Thank you, Ambassador. That's a very thoughtful set of comments from somebody, as they say, "been there, done that," and I appreciate the thoughts.

Professor, thank you very much for joining us. The microphone is yours.

STATEMENT OF PROF. MIKE MOCHIZUKI, DIRECTOR, SIGUR CENTER FOR ASIAN STUDIES, GEORGE WASHINGTON UNIVERSITY, WASHINGTON, DC

Mr. MOCHIZUKI. Thank you very much, Chairman Brownback, for this opportunity to appear before your subcommittee.

We all agree that the North Korean state is a horrific and brutal regime that represses and tortures its own people, and we all agree that this state increasingly engages in international criminal activities to maintain the regime, and that its policies and behavior pose an acute threat to the stability of North East Asia and to our basic security interests and fundamental and moral values. But there is an honest and significant debate and disagreement about how best to deal with North Korea, about whether to and how to incorporate the human-rights issue in our dealings with the North Korean regime.

In a book that Michael O'Hanlon and I recently published on this subject, we articulate and recommend a comprehensive and constructive engagement strategy toward North Korea. Simply put, the strategy involves a more-for- more approach. We would demand more from the North Korean state, but we would also offer more. We would offer regional security assurances, economic aid, technical assistance, and investments in order to entice North Korea to respond positively to a more ambitious agenda that would include conventional arms control and a human-rights dialog, as well as the dismantling of its nuclear weapons and missile programs.

This strategy would seek to fundamentally alter the structure of incentives and disincentives with the North Korean regime. While mobilizing international pressure on North Korea, this approach would seek to steer the regime in a reformist direction by outlining a realistic path out of its present predicament. And we see a human-rights dialog, an improvement in the human-rights situation, in North Korea as an essential component of such a reform trajectory.

The underlying logic or rationale of our more-for-more or grandbargain approach becomes most evident when we compare our approach to other options or alternatives that have been pursued or suggested.

One alternative is to focus primarily on the North Korean nuclear and ballistic missile threat. While recognizing and deploring the atrocities that North Korea commits against its own citizens, proponents of this narrow approach argue that broadening the agenda in our dealings with North Korea will only complicate our negotiations to denuclearize North Korea.

But the recent track record shows the limitations of this narrow approach. North Korea has demonstrated that it will cheat on agreements and use its nuclear programs to blackmail the United States and the international community and extort external aid without fundamentally altering its behavior. We believe the only way to get out of this cycle of cheating, blackmail, and extortion is to encourage North Korea to demilitarize the society and implement economic reforms.

Another alternative approach is what some call "hawkish engagement." This approach involves maximizing international pressure on North Korea by avoiding bilateral negotiations with Pyongyang and insisting on multilateral talks through which China, Russia, and South Korea would join the United States and Japan in criticizing North Korean behavior and policies. Although proponents of this approach are willing to hint, in a piecemeal fashion, about possible positive incentives, such as security assurances and economic aid, they insist that North Korea must first agree to a verifiable and irreversible dismantling and end to its nuclear weapons program. The problem with this approach is that North Korea is unlikely to give up first its strongest diplomatic card before the details of our positive incentives are clearly and publicly articulated. The danger of this approach is that the multilateral talks might yield few positive results and ultimately allow North Korea to engage in stalling tactics while moving forward on the development of nuclear weapons.

A third alternative is to dismiss the possibility of negotiating any kind of workable agreement with North Korea that it will honor. Proponents of this approach argue that what we should be doing is mobilizing an international coalition to squeeze the North Korean regime and ultimately provoke the collapse of the North Korean state.

Although we might all like to see an alternative North Korean state emerge or to see Korean unification after the North Korean state collapses, a squeezing strategy entails major risks.

First of all, there is the strong possibility that the North Korean state will not collapse easily. Instead, a squeezing strategy may cause the North Korean regime to expand its international criminal activities, worsen its abuses against its own people and engage in brinksmanship tactics that increase the danger of miscalculation and military conflict.

Second, an abrupt collapse of the North Korean state could result in political and social chaos, with major negative ramifications for military and human security for which we are ill prepared.

Finally, although China, Russia, and South Korea may be willing to apply diplomatic pressure against North Korea, these countries, and perhaps even Japan, are unlikely to join a squeezing strategy that would aim at provoking a collapse of the North Korean regime.

Critics of Mike O'Hanlon's and my "more-for-more" or "grand-bargain" proposal question whether North Korea would really respond favorably to such an approach. Of course, none of us can say with any certainty how North Korea will respond, because this approach has never been tried.

But there are some indications that it is worth trying this course of action. First, studies of North Korean negotiating behavior suggest that the North Koreans become more responsive and flexible when the agenda is broadened beyond the nuclear issue. But broadening the agenda by proposing up front the vision of a grand bargain does not mean that everything has to be implemented at once. Indeed, the grand bargain can be implemented incrementally on the basis of mutual reciprocity. But to encourage responsiveness and flexibility on the part of North Korea, we recommend that the incentives be articulated in a clear and coherent package, rather than in piecemeal fashion, as the Bush administration is doing today.

Second, since last summer, North Korea has taken some significant, although still limited and inadequate, steps toward economic reforms. Our approach would further encourage this direction.

Third, our approach is more likely to win the support of the major states in the region—China, South Korea, Russia, and especially Japan, if the kidnaping issue is taken up as part of the human-rights dialog. Therefore, proposing the more-for-more bargain would allow us to mobilize the necessary international pressure to compel North Korea to be responsive to our approach. And if, in the end, our approach should fail, then the other countries would be more willing to consider harsher measures against North Korea.

Finally, our approach attempts to get at the root cause of North Korea's economic problems, human rights abuses, its international criminal activities, and its nuclear weapons program—namely, the highly militarized nature of its society. By insisting on significant cuts in its conventional military as part of the Korean Peninsula conventional arms-control process, we could not only reduce the burden that the military imposes on the North Korean economy, but also gradually correct the major distortions of North Korean society. Such an approach, we feel, will work to soften and open up the country to more activities, like humanitarian non-government organizations, international business enterprises, and U.N.-related organizations, and ultimately improve the horrific human-rights situation in that tragic country, and transform this brutal regime.

Thank you very much.

[The prepared statement of Mr. Mochizuki follows:]

PREPARED STATEMENT OF MIKE MOCHIZUKI, DIRECTOR OF THE SIGUR CENTER FOR ASIAN STUDIES, GEORGE WASHINGTON UNIVERSITY, AND MICHAEL O'HANLON, SENIOR FELLOW, FOREIGN POLICY STUDIES, THE SYDNEY STEIN, JR., CHAIR, BROOKINGS INSTITUTE, WASHINGTON, DC

TOWARDS A "GRAND BARGAIN" WITH NORTH KOREA INCLUDING A HUMAN RIGHTS AGENDA

Mr. Chairman, Mr. Ranking Member, other Senators on the committee, it is an honor to appear today to discuss the terrible human rights situation in contemporary North Korea, and the means by which the United States and its regional partners might seek to improve it.

Our argument comes from a book that we recently wrote entitled *Crisis on the Korean Peninsula: How to Deal with a Nuclear North Korea* (McGraw-Hill, 2003) (The book is summarized in the attached article from *The Washington Quarterly* Autumn 2003 issue.) We make a proposal for a new, broader, more demanding negotiating agenda with the DPRK. Some have called this type of approach "more for more"—greater incentives being offered to North Korea to change, but only in exchange for deep reforms in that country going well beyond resolution of the nuclear weapons issue.

We include human rights centrally in the negotiating agenda—in the belief that American values and basic human decency demand it, and in the realpolitik conviction that any country with the current human rights practices of the DPRK cannot be a reliable negotiating partner of the United States. Among our demands are that North Korea allow the return of all Japanese kidnapping victims, and that it begin to engage the international community in a human rights dialogue about its prison camps and other forms of domestic repression that is akin to what we have conducted with China in recent times.

The broader logic of our proposal is simple. We see a negotiation focused only on North Korea's nuclear weapons as posing a catch 22 for the United States. If we offer North Korea major benefits simply for returning to compliance with the 1994 Agreed Framework, we are rewarding proliferant behavior and giving in to a form of extortion. But if we follow the Bush administration's approach and demand that North Korea give up the illicit weapons first, before other issues such as economic

23

development assistance can be discussed, progress is unlikely. Pyongyang probably sees nuclear weapons as perhaps its only real national asset and hence will probably refuse to surrender them without getting a good deal in return. This is a recipe for paralysis in the six-party talks expected to resume later this fall.

The more logical, and it seems to us the more ethical, approach to take in this situation is to offer North Korea economic assistance, a lifting of trade sanctions, and tighter diplomatic ties and stronger security assurances—but only as a way of helping North Korea reform, not as a reward for its recent behavior or for its Stalinist form of government. We can only justify assistance and engagement with North Korea if the process begins to repair an abysmal regime—assuming it is not already beyond repair, as in fact it may be.

A reform agenda must cover all the major issues dividing North Korea from the international community and resulting in the horrible plight of the North Korean people. That means it must address North Korea's oversized military and broken economy. It also means a serious negotiating agenda must compel North Korea to reassess and gradually change its horrendous and fundamentally immoral human rights record.

This type of reform has occurred before within a communist system, most notably in Vietnam and China in recent times. It is hard to achieve, but clearly not impossible. Often, economic reforms lead the way followed by slower political change and improvement in human rights policy. Given the absence of appealing policy alternatives, we can accept such a gradual improvement in North Korean human rights in our judgment, as long as it is crystal clear that we will insist on improvement as part of any deal we negotiate with Pyongyang.

However, attempting such change could also, of course, lead to an uncontrollable sequence of events resulting in such upheaval in North Korea as to produce the demise of that regime. While few in this country would lament such an event, North Korean leaders would surely fear it. That means they would be unlikely to accept such a broad agenda for reform, unless they also faced a stern international community threatening tougher action should the strategy of diplomatic engagement not succeed. Our proposed grand bargain thus requires a continuation of military deterrence and a willingness to use economic as well as even military coercion should diplomacy fail.

By seriously attempting diplomacy first, however, and offering Pyongyang real incentives to change, the United States would improve its ability to convince South Korea, Japan, China, and Russia that tougher measures could be needed if an engagement strategy does not work.

In sum, the broad point here is that even if one swallows disbelief and attempts a serious negotiating agenda with Pyongyang, as we advocate, such an engagement strategy should include a major human rights component. Expectations for rapid change must be realistic, but aspirations must be ambitious, and pressure on North Korea to change must be real. Both American values and hard-headed U.S. foreign policy interests demand it. No narrow negotiation that leaves the present DPRK regime unchanged, but for elimination of its nuclear program, can be expected to produce lasting stability in the region. No such negotiation is in fact even likely to succeed. Ironically, only by enlarging the diplomatic agenda with North Korea do we have any hope of making real progress—or, should talks fail, of convincing our regional security partners to resort to tougher measures if that becomes necessary.

[From The Washington Quarterly • Autumn 2003]

TOWARD A GRAND BARGAIN WITH NORTH KOREA

(By MICHAEL O'HANLON AND MIKE MOCHIZUKI *)

The most promising route to resolve the worsening nuclear crisis in Northeast Asia is for Washington, Tokyo, Seoul, and Beijing to pursue a grand bargain with Pyongyang. These governments need to recognize that North Korean economic atrophy, caused largely by North Korea's excessive conventional military force as well as its failed command-economy system, is at the core of the nuclear crisis and that curing the latter can only be done by recognizing the underlying disease. This grand bargain should be big and bold in scope, addressing the underlying problem while providing bigger and better carrots with the actual potential to entice, together with

*Michael O'Hanlon is a senior fellow at the Brookings Institution in Washington, D.C. Mike Mochizuki is a professor of political science and international affairs at George Washington University. O'Hanlon and Mochizuki are coauthors of *Crisis on the Korean Peninsula: How to Deal with a Nuclear North Korea* (McGraw-Hill, 2003).

24

tough demands on North Korea that go well beyond the nuclear issue. In this comprehensive way, policymakers would provide a road map for the vital and ultimate goal of denuclearizing North Korea. Through the stages of implementation, each side would retain leverage over the other as aid would be provided gradually to the Democratic People's Republic of Korea (DPRK) while the DPRK would cut or eliminate its weapons and reform its economy over time, thus reassuring each side that it was not being hoodwinked.

THE BENEFITS OF THINKING BIG

North Korea is likely to find a broad plan tough and demanding. Such a plan would result in major changes in DPRK security policy as well as its economy and even, to some extent, aspects of domestic policy such as human rights. Yet, such broad road maps are often useful. If the parties lay them out clearly and commit to them early in the process—even if implementation occurs over time—they can help countries on both sides focus on the potentially substantial benefits of a fruitful diplomatic process, thus reducing the odds that negotiations get bogged down in pursuit of marginal advantages on specific issues. Specific pledges can also help countries verify each other's commitment to actual results and thus enhance confidence.[1]

THE FAILURE OF DIPLOMACY DU JOUR

U.S. policy toward North Korea in the last decade has been, for the most part, narrow and tactical, focusing on the crisis du jour rather than on a broader game plan. The 1994 Agreed Framework on North Korea's nuclear program required that the DPRK cease activities that could have given it a nuclear arsenal of 50 weapons by the decade's end; in exchange, the United States and other countries promised to provide North Korea with alternative energy sources. This deal was beneficial within its limited scope, but it failed to address the underlying problem or lead U.S. policymakers to pursue a broader vision beyond the specific attempt to buy out the North Korean missile program later in the decade. Such a tactical approach was perhaps inevitable in the early 1990s, when the Clinton administration was focused on domestic issues and was inexperienced in its foreign policy, as Somalia, Haiti, and Bosnia had shown. As a result of these distractions and inexperience, the Clinton administration had a difficult time at the highest levels of government focusing strategically on North Korea and thus failed to develop an integrated approach for dealing with Pyongyang that combined incentives with threats and deterrence.[2]

A tactical, nuclear-specific focus that involved incentives to alter one specific type of behavior could have been defended as a reasonable approach in the early 1990s. Indeed, until stopped by the Clinton administration, Israel had reportedly been pursuing a deal to compensate North Korea for not selling missiles to Iran.[3] If it made strategic sense for a security-conscious country such as Israel to consider buying out North Korea's missile program, why did it not make sense for the United States and its regional allies to buy out North Korea's even more dangerous nuclear program?

In addition, after the dissolution of the Soviet bloc, many U.S. policymakers expected that North Korea would no longer enjoy the aid or favorable trading arrangements that it needed to survive and would soon collapse, thus obviating the need for a long-term solution. Other policymakers may have expected that concluding a deal on nuclear weapons would naturally lead to a quick thaw in relations on the peninsula without any need to articulate a broader vision. In any event, even if some had wished to articulate such a vision, domestic politics in the United States and in South Korea, where hawks discouraged dealing with the Stalinist regime to the north, stood in the way. Moreover, a tactical, crisis-driven approach to dealing with North Korea did produce some temporary successes, the most significant being the Agreed Framework.

Despite its reasonable logic, however, this approach is not as promising today.[4] President George W. Bush has made it clear that he is opposed to new deals with North Korea on the nuclear issue that smack of blackmail. North Korea has now demonstrated its disinterest in an incremental, slow process of improving relations. It would not have developed its underground uranium-enrichment program—a clear and blatant violation of the Agreed Framework, which required North Korean compliance with the Nuclear Non-Proliferation Treaty—were it content with the benefits of such a patient approach.

In addition, the type of limited engagement pursued over the last decade may have inadvertently encouraged the DPRK to develop a counterproductive habit of using its weapons programs to gain money and diplomatic attention. Whether one views this tendency as extortion or as the desperate actions of a failing regime, the outcome has been the same.

25

Aiming for a big, multifaceted deal might seem counter intuitive when Washington and Pyongyang cannot even sustain a narrow agreement on a specific issue. A recent CSIS report even explicitly argued against making any proposal that included ambitious conventional-arms reductions on the grounds that such broad demands could only be a recipe for stalemate and failure.[5] The 1999 Perry report, drafted by a policy review team led by former secretary of defense William Perry, also took aim at broad proposals, suggesting that they would meet resistance in Pyongyang, which would see any attempt at major reforms as a measure designed to undermine the regime.[6]

The current situation is at an impasse, however; a new idea is needed. The Bush administration's proposal, which demands broad concessions from North Korea, especially on the nuclear weapons front, without offering any concrete incentives in return and which resists bilateral negotiations with Pyongyang, is probably not that new idea. It stands little chance of convincing Pyongyang to change course. Coercion is unlikely to bring about North Korea's collapse or to convince Pyongyang to change its policy quickly enough to prevent a major nuclear crisis in Northeast Asia. Furthermore, this approach elicits little support from key U.S. security partners in the region. South Korea under the Roh government certainly prefers diplomatic engagement over coercion, and although Japan has recently become tougher by stopping North Korean shipping and considering tighter economic sanctions, it still wants to avoid a military crisis that risks war on the Korean peninsula.

Aiming for a larger bargain in which more is offered to North Korea but more is also demanded in return risks little except a bit of money. On the upside, it has the potential to break the current impasse in Northeast Asia, just as broad visions or road maps have guided other recent peace negotiations in the Balkans and the Middle East (with many obvious limitations and setbacks, but some real successes to date as well). The grand bargain approach can benefit both sides. The United States and its allies can reduce the DPRK threat across the board and begin to turn that police state away from a policy of reflexive confrontation and blackmail, while North Korea can gain greater levels of assistance over time and perhaps can begin to reform its economy in the way China did—and as Pyongyang seems to desire, at least occasionally.

Moreover, studies of North Korean negotiating behavior[7] suggest that broader deals may work better than narrow proposals on specific issues. This seemed to be the pattern in the 1993-1994 negotiations leading to the Agreed Framework. Although these talks progressed slowly for a year or so, they produced an accord once the negotiations were broadened beyond the nuclear weapons issue to include energy, economics, security, and diplomatic incentives. Alas, the promises made in this deal were never realized, as all parties (especially the DPRK) put up roadblocks, but the inclusion of these dimensions of the relationship nonetheless helped produce the initial agreement.

In addition to other advantages, a broader approach would also provide the bold initiative that the Roh government suggested that the United States offer to Pyongyang.[8] Without strong cooperation between Seoul and Washington, no plan for dealing with North Korea can work. Indeed, if Pyongyang senses dissension and discord in the U.S.-South Korean alliance, the North Korean government will probably revert to its traditional temptation of trying to split the two allies.

Beyond cooperation with South Korea, a grand bargain proposal can make U.S. policy much more palatable to other key regional players—Japan and China. Collaboration among these four countries in their basic approach to resolving the North Korean problem is essential to prevent Pyongyang from being tempted to play one government off against the others, as it often has done in the past, and to enable these four countries to work together to pursue their common goals.[9] Yet, they will not unite behind a policy that begins with hard-line measures; in particular, South Korea and China will consider taking a tough stance against Pyongyang only after serious diplomatic steps have clearly been attempted and have failed. Uniting the four players is thus the best way both to improve the prospects for diplomacy and a successful coercive strategy, should that diplomacy fail.

MAKING IT WORK

For the grand bargain to work, both carrots and sticks are needed—incentives as well as resolute deterrence and even threats if need be. Beyond the nuclear issue, such a grand bargain must also address the broader problems on the Korean peninsula—most notably North Korea's oversized military and undersized economy, as well as a horrible human rights record that is repressive even by Communist standards.

26

BALANCING CARROTS AND STICKS

A policy that uses carrots and sticks is not necessarily a contradictory one. Although the world should not give Pyongyang substantial aid and other benefits simply to appease a dangerous leader or to solve an immediate security crisis, the United States and its allies can and should be generous if North Korea is prepared to eliminate its nuclear weapons programs, transform the broader security situation on the peninsula, reform its economy, and even begin to change its society. Doing so would not show weakness but rather provide a way to solve—not postpone—an important security problem by changing the fundamental nature of the adversary.

Moreover, depending on the particular circumstances surrounding negotiations, the grand bargain's strategic use of carrots can help retain the threat of a military strike against Yongbyon as a last resort. Although Washington has been unable to convince Seoul of the need for such a threat today, that situation could change. A committed, initial attempt at diplomacy, including the offer of numerous inducements for North Korea, would give the United States a better chance of getting its regional allies to support a military threat as a last resort. By providing more carrots, the U.S. government might thus gain greater support for the possible, subsequent use of a stick.[10]

Any military strike at North Korea's nuclear reactors and plutonium reprocessing facilities at its Yongbyon site north of Pyongyang would be extremely risky in light of the possibility that a larger war would result. Furthermore, a military strike would probably fail to destroy or render unusable many of North Korea's spent fuel rods, meaning that the DPRK might still manufacture one or more weapons even after an attack. (Although some may be concerned about direct radioactive fallout, studies conducted by the Pentagon in the early 1990s concluded that radioactive release would probably be quite limited, unless an operational nuclear reactor with heavily irradiated fuel was struck.)

Nevertheless, the preemption option would arguably be preferable to an unchecked, large-scale DPRK nuclear program, if someday that was the only alternative. Such a threat was credible when the Clinton administration made it in 1994 because South Korea did not fundamentally object. The Bush administration can probably make it credible again by pursuing better diplomacy and better coordination with Seoul, Tokyo, and Beijing. A military strike is, of course, not likely to destroy either the DPRK's hidden uranium-enrichment program or the bomb or two that North Korea might have already, nor would military action destroy any additional plutonium moved from Yongbyon prior to the attack. Nevertheless, a strike could destroy the DPRK's nuclear reactors at the site, entomb the associated plutonium, and destroy the reprocessing facility—all with limited risk of radioactive fallout, according to former secretary of defense Perry and former assistant secretary Ashton Carter.[11]

North Korea's true hard-liners may fear the Bush administration to such an extent that they argue against giving up their nuclear program at present—which also may have been the case during the Clinton administration.[12] The grand bargain proposal may be able to convince the DPRK to abandon its nuclear programs gradually, however, through a combination of reassurances and inducements.[13] Kim Jong Il has demonstrated sufficient interest in engaging with the outside world as well as in exploring economic reforms—evidenced by the creation of special economic zones, the recent liberalization of prices, and other tentative but real steps to try some of what China and Vietnam have successfully attempted in recent decades. The United States and other countries should seriously test his willingness to go further.

Moreover, Kim Jong Il's position within North Korea now appears strong. He has used purges and promotions to produce a top officer corps loyal to him, and the likelihood that military commanders think that they have a solution of their own to solve North Korea's economic problems is slim. If a proposed package deal were to address the country's core security concerns while providing a real opportunity for recovery and greater international engagement, North Korea may very well take the idea seriously.[14] A grand bargain that allowed North Korea to surrender its nuclear capabilities gradually while allowing it to keep some fraction of its conventional weaponry near the demilitarized zone (DMZ) just might persuade Pyongyang to get on board.

The DPRK might prefer to have both aid and nuclear weapons, but the United States should try to force North Korea to choose between the two.[15] This is in fact the crux of the logic behind the grand bargain approach: that North Korea can be forced to choose and that it can probably be induced to make the right, peaceful choice.

The allies would not let down their military guard at any point during the proposed process nor would a failed experiment cause any other irrevocable harm. Even a failed effort to negotiate a grand bargain would at least temporarily ice the larger, visible part of the DPRK's nuclear program because no negotiations would proceed unless Pyongyang allowed monitoring of its program and froze it as well. Further, because the aid would be provided mostly in kind, not in cash, it would by itself do little to prop up a desperate regime with the hard currency it so desperately craves.

Going Beyond the Nuclear Issue

By not fixating on just the nuclear program, ironically, a grand bargain is more likely ultimately to denuclearize North Korea and, most importantly, prevent any further development of North Korea's nuclear inventory. The proposed plan would begin by rapidly restoring fuel oil shipments and promising no immediate use of U.S. force if North Korea agreed to freeze its nuclear activities, particularly plutonium production and reprocessing at Yongbyon, while negotiations are under way. These steps would simply ensure that neither party had to negotiate under duress.

As for its main substance, the approach would then seek to strike a deal on nuclear weapons. The proposal would replace North Korea's nuclear facilities at Yongbyon with conventional power sources and include rigorous monitoring of North Korea's nuclear-related sites as well as short-notice challenge inspections at places where outside intelligence suspected nuclear-related activity.

Given North Korea's concerns about the Bush administration's doctrine of preemption and the success of military operations against Iraq, convincing the DPRK to give up all its nuclear capabilities immediately might not be feasible.[16] In fact, it might take several years, perhaps even until the end of the decade, to reach that final goal. The United States could accept any deal, however, that could immediately freeze the DPRK's nuclear activities verifiably and then quickly begin to get fuel rods out of North Korea.

Beyond nuclear issues, both sides would cut the overall number of conventional forces as well as accompany those cuts with a commitment by South Korea, China, Japan, and the United States to help North Korea gradually restructure its economy. Cuts of 50 percent or more in conventional weaponry would reduce the threat that North Korea's artillery and rocket forces currently pose to South Korea, particularly to nearby Seoul. Unlike some proposals, the grand bargain would not entail the North Korean withdrawal of all its conventional capabilities from the DMZ. North Korea almost surely considers its forward-deployed forces necessary to deter South Korea and the United States. Hence, the DPRK cannot realistically be expected to surrender both its weapons of mass destruction (WMD) and its conventional deterrent.

The principal purpose of these conventional reductions actually would be as much economic as military. Offering aid tied to cuts in conventional arms makes more economic sense than buying out nuclear and missile programs. Secretary of Defense Donald Rumsfeld recently convincingly argued that the real solution to North Korea's problems is for the country to move toward a market economy, because that approach has worked for other Communist states in East Asia, notably China and Vietnam.[17] North Korea may actually be planning secretly to make cuts in its conventional forces anyway.[18] A combination of cuts in DPRK forces and economic reforms in the country stands the best chance of producing stabilizing and desirable results.

If Pyongyang agreed to such reductions, North Korea's economy would benefit twice: by a reduction in the size and cost of its military and by obtaining greater technical and economic aid from Japan, South Korea, the United States, and perhaps China (as well as the lifting of U.S. trade sanctions). Specifically, such a deal should reduce North Korea's military expenditures substantially, helping reform the country's economy and increasing the likelihood that aid is used productively. North Korea's conventional military forces comprise one million individuals and are backed up by large reserve forces as well as a large arms industry. This situation suggests that the lion's share of North Korea's defense budget, which represents 20-30 percent of its gross domestic product, is consumed by conventional forces; therefore, reducing them should be a main focus of any reform proposal. External aid can help in that process.

This policy would reduce the core threat that has existed in Korea for half a century, while offering at least some hope that economic reform in the DPRK might begin to succeed. Given this economic logic and rationale, it would only make sense to keep giving aid so long as North Korea continued down the path of economic reform. China could provide technical help, in light of its experiences over the last 25 years in gradually introducing entrepreneurial activity into a Communist economy.

China's experience could also offer reassurance—surely important to North Korean leaders—that it is possible to reform a command economy without losing political power in the process. Even though most Americans would surely prefer to see North Korea's corrupt and ruthless government fall, pursuing a policy that would achieve that outcome does not seem realistic without incurring huge security risks and exacting an enormous humanitarian toll on the North Korean people—nor would China and South Korea likely support it under current circumstances. Moreover, by accepting this grand bargain proposal, North Korea would be agreeing to at least a gradual and soft, or "velvet," form of regime change, even if Kim Jong Il were to retain power throughout the process.

Additional elements of the grand bargain would include North Korean commitments to:

- continue to refrain from terrorism;
- permanently return all kidnapping victims to Japan;
- participate in a human rights dialogue, similar to China in recent years;
- end DPRK counterfeiting and drug smuggling activities;
- sign and implement its obligations under the chemical weapons and biological weapons conventions; and
- stop exports and production of ballistic missiles.

For its part of the grand bargain, the United States would offer numerous benefits beyond economic and energy assistance, none of which would require a change in the U.S. government's fundamental regional policies. The White House would:

- commence diplomatic ties with North Korea;
- end economic sanctions;
- remove North Korea's name from the list of state sponsors of terrorism;
- give a binding promise not to be the first to use WMD;
- provide a nonaggression pledge—a promise not to attack North Korea first with any types of weaponry for any purpose (and perhaps even an active security guarantee if North Korea wished, akin to what the United States provides to its allies); and
- sign a formal peace treaty ending the Korean War.

BREAKING THE STALEMATE

After a decade of issue-by-issue and initially fruitful negotiations, a broad vision is now needed to resolve the impasse on the Korean peninsula. This idea must address the underlying cause of the problem—North Korea's economic and societal collapse, together with its failed experiment in communism and its *juche* system of self-reliance—as well as the immediate nuclear symptoms of that disease.

Although couched in broad and ambitious terms, the proposed road map could be put into effect gradually. Intrusive nuclear inspections typically take months or longer, reductions in conventional forces take at least a couple of years, and development programs take even longer. Thus, the concept is grand in its intent and scope, but implementation of the policy need not be rushed. In fact, the need for gradual implementation would provide each side with leverage over the other.

The United States and its partners would continue to provide aid and economic support only if North Korea upheld its end of the bargain. Similarly, security guarantees would be contingent on complete compliance with denuclearization demands as well as other elements of the proposal. For its part, North Korea would not have to give up all its nuclear potential until it gained a number of concrete benefits, and the government would not have to keep reducing conventional forces unless outside powers continued to provide assistance.

Although reductions in conventional forces are the linchpin of the grand bargain's success, numerous additional key elements are involved, the most important of which is a broad approach to economic reform in North Korea. There is reason to believe that the economic reform model that worked in China starting about a quarter century ago can work in Korea today, although each case is distinct. If that is the case, a grand bargain could do much more than address an acute nuclear security problem; the approach could begin to transform what has been one of the world's most troubled and dangerous regions for decades.

29

NOTES

[1] Richard N. Haass and Meghan L. O'Sullivan, "Terms of Engagement: Alternatives to Punitive Policies," *Survival* 42, no. 2 (summer 2000): 120-121.

[2] Leon V. Sigal, *Disarming Strangers: Nuclear Diplomacy with North Korea* (Princeton, N.J.: Princeton University Press, 1998), pp. 52-65.

[3] Ibid.,pp.66-67.

[4] See Morton I. Abramowitz and James T. Laney, *Testing North Korea: The Next Stage in U.S. and ROK Policy* (New York: Council on Foreign Relations, 2001), www.cfr.org/pdf/Korea_TaskForce2.pdf (accessed June 19, 2003). For more recent arguments along similar lines, see Brent Scowcroft and Daniel Poneman, "Korea Can't Wait," *Washington Post,* February 16, 2003; Samuel R. Berger and Robert L. Gallucci, "Two Crises, No Back Burner," *Washington Post,* December 31, 2002; William S. Cohen, "Huffing and Puffing Won't Do," *Washington Post,* January 7, 2003; Ashton B. Carter, "Alternatives to Letting North Korea Go Nuclear," testimony before the Senate Committee on Foreign Relations, Washington, D.C., March 6, 2003; Sonni Efron, "Experts Call for N. Korea Dialogue," *Los Angeles Times,* March 7, 2003 (citing testimony by Robert Einhorn); Morton Abramowitz and James Laney, "A Letter from the Independent Task Force on Korea to the Administration," November 26, 2002, www.cfr.org/publication.php?id5304 (accessed June 18, 2003); "Turning Point in Korea: New Dangers and New Opportunities for the United States," February 2003, www.ciponline.org/asia/taskforce.pdf (accessed June 18, 2003) (report of the Task Force on U.S. Korea policy).

[5] CSIS International Security Program Working Group, "Conventional Arms Control on the Korean Peninsula," Washington, D.C., August 2002, www.csis.org/isp/conv_armscontrol.pdf (accessed June 18, 2003). See Alan D. Romberg and Michael D. Swaine, "The North Korea Nuclear Crisis: A Strategy for Negotiation," *Arms Control Today* 33, no. 4 (May 2003): 4-7.

[6] William J. Perry, "Review of United States Policy Toward North Korea: Findings and Recommendations," Washington, D.C., October 12, 1999, www.state.gov/www/regions/eap/991012_northkorea_rpt.html (accessed June 18, 2003).

[7] Scott Snyder, *Negotiating on the Edge* (Washington, D.C.: U.S. Institute of Peace, 1999), pp. 58-60, 143-153; Sigal, *Disarming Strangers,* pp. 52-65, 78.

[8] See "S. Korea Urges U.S. Initiative for North," *Washington Post,* March 29, 2003.

[9] See Snyder, *Negotiating on the Edge,* pp. 149-150.

[10] Gary Samore, "The Korean Nuclear Crisis," *Survival* 45, no. 1 (spring 2003): 19-22.

[11] See Ashton B. Carter and William J. Perry, "Back to the Brink," *Washington Post,* October 20, 2002.

[12] See Philip W. Yun, "The Devil We Know in N. Korea May Be Better Than the Ones We Don't," *Los Angeles Times,* May 7, 2003.

[13] See Michael Armacost, Daniel I. Okimoto, and Gi-Wook Shin, "Addressing the North Korea Nuclear Challenge," Asia/Pacific Research Center, Institute for International Studies, Stanford University, April 15, 2003, www.asck.org/reports/APARC_Brief_1_2003.pdf (accessed June 18, 2003).

[14] See Kongdan Oh and Ralph C. Hassig, *North Korea Through the Looking Glass* (Washington, D.C.: Brookings Institution, 2000), pp. 114-124.

[15] For a similar argument, see Joseph S. Nye, "Bush Faces a Tougher Test in N. Korea," *Boston Globe,* May 7, 2003.

[16] See Doug Struck, "Citing Iraq, N. Korea Signals Hard Line on Weapons Issues," *Washington Post,* March 30, 2003; James Brooke, "North Korea Watches War and Wonders What's Next," *New York Times,* March 31, 2003.

[17] Bill Sammon, "N. Korea 'Solution' a Market Economy," *Washington Times,* May 14, 2003.

[18] The North Korean statement of June 9, 2003, that justified its nuclear weapons programs as a way to compensate for reductions in conventional military forces suggests such an inference. David Sanger, "North Korea Says It Seeks to Develop Nuclear Arms," *New York Times,* June 10, 2003, p. A9.

Senator BROWNBACK. Thank you very much, professor.

And I want to thank all the panelists.

First, Mr. Hawk, this is the best detailed description and the marrying together that I've seen of the stories that I have heard, the interviews that I have done with a number of refugees coming out of North Korea, and then matching them with the satellite photography. I think it's an excellent contribution that you're making to the debate of something the North Koreans have denied for years. They just say, "Well, it doesn't exist," and you hear all this testimony coming out from people and then marrying the two up, I think it was a great contribution. I deeply appreciate that.

But why is it taking us so long, in the international community, to recognize the size and scale of this horrific gulag system and deaths that are taking place in North Korea? In this day and age, it seems like this is something we should be on top of immediately. Why is it taking us so long?

Mr. HAWK. I think primarily because of the extreme isolation of North Korea. Up until 2 years ago, they had relations, diplomatic relations, only with Soviet bloc countries. It's only within the last 2 years that you have the EU establishing diplomatic relations and the kind of talks that that allows, and it's only within the last 2 years that you have a large enough body of former refugees, including former prisoners who have obtained asylum in South Korea, so that you have a critical mass there now of testimony and of evidence. Previously, you had Kang Chul Hwan's prison memoirs of Yodok, and you had Soon Ok Lee's book about "The Eyes of the Tailless Animals," of her prison memoirs at Kaechon kyo-hwa-so, and you had a few other people who had given interviews in Seoul and also in Washington. But it's really only within the last 2 years that you have enough—a critical mass of people who have obtained asylum. And, you know, they escaped into China and have to make their way to Mongolia or Hong Kong, most of them all the way down through Southern China, down through Burma, Vietnam, or Laos, into Cambodia, into Thailand, where they fly from Bangkok to Seoul and seek asylum in South Korea. So it's actually taken several years, or several months, for these former North Koreans to get to a place where journalists and human-rights researchers can get at them, and that's only been possible in the last 2 years.

So I think it's largely because of the self-imposed isolation of the regime, which didn't have diplomats there, outside the Soviet bloc, and didn't allow journalists in, or academics, and certainly not human-rights investigators.

Senator BROWNBACK. When did large-scale refugee flights start out of North Korea, Mr. Hawk?

Mr. HAWK. In the mid 1990s or the late 1990s, with the height of the famine crisis, when the production and distribution system broke down. And 1995 is the year often cited—that's when the North Koreans admitted they had a problem. But from that point on, when the distribution centers were no longer handing out food, and the production centers were no longer functioning and paying people to work, that you had people either fleeing North Korea to China to find food, or else sending a member of their family up to China to get a job to earn income to send the money back to North Korea so the family could obtain some food. So that only started in the mid- to late-1990s, and then it's really about 2000 when you start getting these people making their way to South Korea.

Senator BROWNBACK. I'm going to ask all of you gentlemen, and start with you, Mr. Hawk, on this. You've all stated that we need a human-rights portfolio in the package of negotiations that are taking place with North Korea and the surrounding countries and the United States.

But let me pose the question to you in reverse. What are the dangers, if any, in failing to include human rights on the negotiating agenda? Say we just stay on a narrow issue that this is about nuclear weapons and the proliferation of nuclear weapons, and that's it. What is the danger of not including human rights in a negotiating portfolio?

Mr. HAWK. To the extent to which I understand the North Korean negotiating position, they don't want only security arrangements. They want a security guarantee, but they also want large amounts of foreign aid, and they want lots of goodies, and they want foreign investment. And they want to be able to get investment from South Korea into various production zones from which goods are shipped to Europe and the United States, which is how most of the other countries in East Asia have developed and become prosperous. I think North Korea wants to join the queue of states of building toys and electronics et cetera, and shipping them to the United States. So if these issues that come up in the negotiations, then I don't see how you cannot also raise the issue of labor standards. I mean, we're not supposed to import slave or prison-labor-made goods anyway, and—I hope Congress will encourage the U.S. negotiators not to envision a situation where production for export zones are developed while domestic production is based on prison, slave, and forced labor.

I believe it's the North Koreans who don't want to accept a purely security tradeoff. I think their intent is to ask for a lot more than that. And as long as that is the case, then it seems that the "basket-three" equivalent should be put on the table. The humanitarian and human-rights considerations—the elements that are enumerated in the conclusions and appendices of the report—provide the details and specifics of the human-rights dialog that Mike's book talks about.

Senator BROWNBACK. Ambassador Palmer.

Ambassador PALMER. Well, I think that the greatest danger is the nature of their regime does not change under those circumstances. If you continue to have a regime that's closed, that's involved with other terrorist states and encouraging terrorism—that is, exporting weapons to places like Pakistan, et cetera, or the delivery of weapons of mass destruction. I mean, unless you change the basic nature of the North Korean situation, the political situation there, internally, it will continue to be a very dangerous state. Even if you can get verified restrictions on their nuclear weapons program for 1 year or 2 years, you'd never know when they're going to fall off the wagon even on that, and plus they may go ahead with BW programs or CW programs, or God knows what.

So I think the only real secure guarantee that we will ever have that this regime is going to cease being the kind of menace to its neighbors and for that world that it is today is to change the regime. I mean, it's simple, to me.

Senator BROWNBACK. Professor.

Mr. MOCHIZUKI. I generally agree with that. Unless the regime is fundamentally transformed, I don't think that even if we do reach an agreement on the nuclear issue, a narrow agreement, that there will continue to be the cycle of cheating, blackmail, and extortion. And really it is an agreement that is bound to fail, like the one in 1994. So if you are going to tackle the nuclear issue, then you have to get at the fundamental problem, the nature of the regime.

Senator BROWNBACK. The North Koreans frequently employ a strategy of brinkmanship. And, particularly, Ambassador Palmer, I want you to address this in negotiations, given your background in the Soviet Union, Eastern Europe, fall of communism at that point in time. Are there any parallels to what you saw at that point in time in the brinkmanship versus what you're seeing now in the brinkmanship of North Korea? And are there any lessons that we can derive from what history would teach us then, to now?

Ambassador PALMER. Yes, I think there are. The historical periods are kind of a little bit confusing, but, for example, when Khrushchev was threatening us with nuclear devastation, which he did quite openly, what it really indicated was not that he wanted to launch nuclear weapons against us, but he was desperate, in terms of his own domestic situation. And, of course, he was ultimately pushed out.

I think that Gorbachev, who I knew directly—Gorbachev, there's some interesting—when you look at Kim Jong Il and what he's been going in the last 2 years, there's some interesting parallels between Gorbachev and Kim Jong Il. I think Gorbachev recognized and certainly talked with George Schultz and with President Reagan in my presence about—he didn't know what to do. You know, this was a man who was really adrift. He had tons of questions, and no answers. That's my sense of Kim Jong Il, that he's been traveling to Russia, traveling to China, trying to find answers. He's dabbled, he's put his toe in the water of a little bit of reform, which has unleashed all kinds of bad stuff, as well as some good stuff.

And so I think it's very much in our interest to engage him directly. Him. Not the system or the regime or the government, but him. And in my book, I go on at some length about how to do this, both through carrots and sticks. I think it's important to talk with him about his alternatives. His alternatives are really that he goes down in history as a criminal and maybe ends up in jail or maybe even is dead, gets killed, like Ceaucescu, or he can cooperate with this transition, end up with a villa in Geneva, and, you know, have a nice life.

So, you know, but we need to get close enough, somebody has to get close enough to him, and I would argue we ought to open an embassy in Pyongyang, which could distribute radios, so Norbert's balloons aren't the only way of getting radios in there. We ought to have an embassy there doing what our embassy in Havana is doing, giving out radios, which is the best thing that embassy, or office, in Havana, has ever done. And we could do that in Pyongyang. But you need to be on the ground.

So I think that we ought to go in there. I very much agree with David's point that they want a big, broad agenda, and we ought to run in there and say, "Terrific. We want a big, broad agenda, too." I think he's desperate. I think he knows he's in trouble, and we ought to be confident enough to use our strength when he's in trou-

33

ble. And our strength is our values and our ideology. That's our strength. That's where we're on the side of the North Korean people. We ought to get in there, open up the place, and bring him down.

Senator BROWNBACK. Professor, would you respond to that same question?

Mr. MOCHIZUKI. Yes. I mean, it's definitely true that Kim Jong Il and his father engaged in brinksmanship tactics.

But I think the problem is, is that our present piecemeal approach gives the initiative to North Korea and allows them to use brinksmanship in order to gain diplomatic leverage.

Ambassador Palmer talked about a carrot-and-stick approach. I would argue that what we need is a sledgehammer-and-steaks approach, that we really maximize our international pressure, and that means getting not just Russia and South Korea and Japan onboard, but China onboard, but, at the same time, offering major incentives, like steaks. I mean, I think that's the only way you get out of this cycle of North Korea seizing the initiative by using brinksmanship and we basically pursue a reactive policy.

Senator BROWNBACK. Gentlemen, thank you very much for your insightfulness on a very difficult topic, and I appreciate it. And I appreciate particularly your policy recommendations that you brought here today.

Now I'd like to invite the second panel to the table.

Ms. Sandy Rios, who is the chairperson of the North Korean Freedom Coalition. She serves as president of Concerned Women of America, the nation's largest public-policy women's organization, with half a million members nationwide. She currently hosts Concerned Women Today, a daily radio program. She has an audience of nearly a million listeners a week.

Mr. Kumar is advocacy director for Asia and the Pacific at Amnesty International. He is—on a personal note, many in the human-rights community continue to miss your former colleague, Mike Jay—a passionate advocate for North Korean refugees and, as I understand it, a key contributor to Amnesty International's report. I hope this hearing serves to advance the goals of Mike, as well.

And then we have Mr. Joel Charny. He's vice president for Policy, Refugees International, recently returned from a trip to northeast China, where he had an opportunity to meet with and interview a number of North Korean refugees.

I welcome all of you to the panel here today.

And, Ms. Rios, please proceed with your testimony.

STATEMENT OF SANDY RIOS, CHAIRMAN, NORTH KOREA FREEDOM COALITION, AND PRESIDENT, CONCERNED WOMEN FOR AMERICA, WASHINGTON, DC

Ms. RIOS. Senator Brownback, it's a great privilege to be able to testify for you today. And I have to say, though, more than an honor; it's a responsibility for me, and I'd like to explain that.

As you said, I am the president of Concerned Women for America, but I also wear the hat of chairman of the North Korea Freedom Coalition. While most of you in this room were grappling with the horrors of September 11, 2001, I and a few companions were traveling, unaware, in that dark and isolated land known as North Korea. We had crossed the bridge over the Tumen River by foot under the watchful eye of armed guards the day before, visited schools, seen their children perform with robotic excellence, enter the Presidential concubine's gambling casino and traveled around a vacation island viewing herds of seals from a rented speedboat. That's what we were doing as the World Center Trade Towers fell, and it wasn't until 24 hours after the fact, when we passed back across that bridge into northern Manchuria, that a restaurant owner told us the news. One of my companions from New York City used a satellite phone to call his wife, who then confirmed the dreadful news. We were then stranded in Beijing for several days and were finally able to make it out and back home, only by going through Japan.

Our journey had begun in China, where our assignment was to interview North Korean refugees who had escaped and were hiding in northern Manchuria. Much of them had fled across the river, desperate for food. Much like the famed escapes of the oppressed East Germans over the Berlin Wall, the stories are legion of the heroism and determination that lack of freedom drives men and women to in this part of the world. The difference in the peoples lies in the end result. For the East Germans, to survive the escape was to be free. But for the North Koreans, to survive the escape was to eat, yes, but then to enter a twilight zone of existence that no person on this Earth should have to endure.

It is the Chinese and ethnic Korean Christians who greet the refugees with rice and the love of God. They open their homes at great risk, knowing that their own fates will be determined by the dangers they dare to embrace. They take these people in willingly, sacrificially, and their faith is a testimony to the power of God in the face of abject evil.

I sat on the floor with four young boys and their plump and smiling surrogate mother in the kitchen at her small home in a village up in the mountains. I said "young boys" because they appeared to be prepubescent teenagers, but, in reality, they were 16 and 17 years old. Their bodies were underdeveloped and malnourished due to the famine and to the fact that Kim Jong Il routes humanitarian aid to the military while starving his own people. They were told in school, incidentally, that there was no rice because the Americans had sunk the ships bringing in the food. Three of them, friends, had just recently swum across the Tumen River separating the two countries in a valiant and courageous effort to get food and, in one boy's case, to take the enormous risk of bringing some of it back to his starving mother.

The boy who was planning to make that treacherous return trip was animated and smiling. He was filled with mission and purpose. And after telling us that he had learned about God in this loving sanctuary, our interpreter asked him if he was going to go back and declare his faith.

With refreshing candor characteristic of his colorful personality, he said softly, "I don't have that much faith yet."

Another one huddled beside me with the twisted, silent countenance only a trauma victim can display. He talked quietly about their dangerous swim across the river and how in one moment he thought he was going to die, how the other two boys encouraged him on, and how they had persevered to the shore for freedom, still with no expression, the voice subdued.

The woman who had taken them in was constantly moving about, touching and hugging and feeding them. She was a Christian, one of the band of brave souls who are risking their own lives and well-being to help the people that no one wants, the North Korean refugees.

The boys were not permitted to leave the house, they couldn't go to school, work, or play, because if caught they would be sent back and summarily executed. The Chinese Government doesn't want them. The South Korean Government doesn't want them, and the current U.S. policy severely limits sanctuary here. There is no place to go.

As we tried to leave this mountain hideaway, neighbors came out of their houses, watching, not with innocent curiosity, but with the intention of spying and reporting on their rebellious neighbor. We shuddered to think of her fate as we pulled away.

The next day, we ventured into a town on the border and tried, at least, in spite of passing an unexpected prison chain gang, to enter a Chinese apartment discretely. We quickly climbed the steps to the top floor and entered silently. We were ushered into a, sort of, family room, where five more refugees were sitting, along with the apartment dweller, another Christian and his wife who had opened their home. Once we entered the room, the doorbell rang, and an electric wave of tension surged through all of us. The man rushed to shut the door to the room, and another watched nervously out the window, and we felt, in that moment, the dread fear the Chinese and North Koreans live with daily. Our hearts pounded as we realized that it was a false alarm.

I proceeded to interview two of the refugees. One was a young mother, who had fled across the Tumen River herself to get food for her husband and baby. She was aided, once again, by Christ's followers, who gave her rice and a small bible, after which she made the dangerous trip back with her treasure, she was subsequently caught and put in prison. And hatred of Christianity in North Korea was so great that if you are caught with a Bible not only do they punish you, but your parents and children, three generations. She was waiting for her sentence in the prison when she chose to jump from the top floor, an attempt to kill herself and hopefully save her family. She fell in a broken heap and was left for dead, but she was not dead. As I sat beside her on the floor, I saw the mangled bones in her feet and legs juxtaposed to her otherwise beautiful body and face. At 24, her life was over. She had lost her husband; her child; she could not leave this apartment, except in the dark of night; could not hold a job; had no future and no hope.

Next, I turned to a 12-year-old girl hovering on a couch. Another child/adult wearing the unmistakable countenance of trauma, no expression; just a deep, deep furrow in her brow. Words without emotion devoid of eye contact. She told how for the past several years she had been hiking daily up into the mountains, a ten-kilometer walk one way, to spend the day picking branches off trees. She would then bundle them together, drag them back the same ten kilometers to sell them for the American equivalent of 25 cents in order to feed her sick father and little brother. Somehow she had escaped, but, in the process, her little brother had disappeared. It was in reliving that moment that she broke down and could not go on with her story.

When I left that room, with those people, fully comprehending the risk that they had taken not only to escape but to allow me to come and hear their stories, I vowed to them on that day that they had not taken that risk in vain—that I would make sure their stories were told so that the whole world could hear.

I was a radio talk-show host at the time, and confident I could go back and accomplish that. I was reporting for my new job here in Washington on October 15, but my plan was to use the 2-weeks I had left to expose the evil I had seen. Little did I know that my country would be attacked, leaving me and my companions stranded in Beijing, and that that would cut my remaining time on the air so short I wouldn't have the ability to do what I had earnestly promised. It grieved me to let them down in that way, but I couldn't see how my duties as president of Concerned Women for America would ever intersect with their needs.

Leave it to the gracious God that I serve to find a way. The North Korea Freedom Coalition came about quite unexpectedly. My selection as chairman, an equal surprise, but it is a surprise I welcome, and it is with the passion of one who has seen the evil of Kim Jong Il and his regime that I lead and will continue to lead this group.

I lived in Berlin, Germany, during the height of the cold war. I traveled regularly through Checkpoint Charlie into East Berlin and observed the palpable oppression of the East German people. I've been to Vietnam, to China several times, and to Russia before the breakup of the Soviet Union.

I have tasted and smelled the evils of oppression, but I can tell you that I don't think anything matches the horror of life in North Korea. That's why I stand to speak and, if necessary, shout their cause for them today.

The North Korea Freedom Coalition is a bipartisan coalition of religious, human-rights, non-governmental Korean and American organizations whose prime purpose is to bring freedom to the North Korean people and to ensure that the human-rights component of the U.S. and world policy toward North Korea receive priority attention.

We're a coalition of both the ideological left and right, ranging from the Salvation Army USA to the Religious Action Center of Reform Judaism headed by David Saperstein, because on issues of human need and desperation we can most certainly agree.

We are strong supporters of the North Korea Freedom Act of 2003, as you know, Senator Brownback, the soon to be bipartisan act that will promote human rights, democracy, and development in North Korea. The provisions contained in the act will provide safe harbor for North Korean refugees, provide ways to get information and food to those starving for both, monitor the death camps so well detailed in David Hawk's report, and make sure that not one American dollar is spent to build another gulag. Further, any negotiating with the North Korean regime that says, "You can continue to starve and torture your people as long as you dismantle the weapons of mass destruction," is as unacceptable as it is un-American.

And while we wish no harm to our South Korean friends, we also stand to remind them that it is equally unacceptable for them to prop up a regime that is starving and torturing their relatives to the north, because the consequences of saving them would be too costly.

We will encourage our government to help South Korea absorb the difficulties that may come, but only the extent that the South ceases to aid and abet the murderous regime of the North.

Not only are we determined to get information and freedom into North Korea, we are determined to get the word out, in the West, of the brutality and starvation of the North Korean people by their "Dear Leader." We believe that, by God's grace, the net effect of such a movement can be much the same as the fall of both the Soviet Union and the Berlin Wall, no shots fired, just freedom imploding.

President Bush has led the way on this issue by boldly and rightly declaring North Korea part of an "axis of evil." This is no time for the faint of heart or spineless appeasers. This is a time for Americans of all political stripes to unite for a noble purpose: to bring freedom, food, and wholeness to the suffering people of North Korea.

Senator Brownback, one additional word. We have been able to, I guess, find a lot of resonation with this piece of legislation with unexpected groups here in the country, and one of those is South Korean students in America. Let me just mention a few groups that have signed onto this legislation. The Korean American Students at Yale, the MIT Asian Christian Fellowship, the Brandeis Korean Students Association, the UC-Berkeley Students Praying for North Korea, and Korea-American Student Association at Stanford, and there's a ton of others. South Korean churches in this country are mightily stirred by this, and they're coming out in support of this act. In fact, we've received petitions containing 6,438 signatures of Korean Americans who support this legislation from 93 Korean American churches in 18 different states in the nation, and this, sir, is just the beginning.

Thank you so much for this time.

[The prepared statement of Ms. Rios follows:]

PREPARED STATEMENT OF SANDY RIOS, CHAIRMAN, NORTH KOREA FREEDOM COALITION AND PRESIDENT, CONCERNED WOMEN FOR AMERICA, WASHINGTON, DC

Mr. Chairman and members of the committee, I consider it a great honor to testify before you today, but more than an honor, a responsibility. I will explain. I am the President of Concerned Women for America, the largest public policy women's organization in the country, but I come before you today wearing a different hat, that of Chairman of the North Korea Freedom Coalition.

While most of you were grappling with the horrors of September 11, 2001, I and a few companions were traveling unaware in that dark and isolated land known as North Korea. We had crossed the bridge over the Tumen River by foot under the watchful eye of armed guards the day before, visited their schools, seen their children perform with robotic excellence, entered the presidential concubine's gambling casino and traveled around a "vacation island," viewing herds of seals from a rented speedboat. That's what we were doing as the World Center Trade Towers fell, and it wasn't until 24 hours after the fact, when we passed back across the bridge into Northern Manchuria, that a restaurant owner told us the news. One of my companions from New York City used a satellite phone to call his wife who confirmed the dreadful news.

We were then stranded in Beijing for several days and were finally able to make it out and back home only by going through Japan.

Our journey had begun in China where our assignment was to interview North Korean refugees who had escaped and were hiding in Northern Manchuria. Most of them had fled across the river desperate for food. Much like the famed escapes of the oppressed East Germans over the Berlin Wall, the stories are legion of the heroism and determination that lack of freedom drives men and women to in this part of the world. The difference in the peoples lies in the end result. For the East Germans, to survive the escape was to be free. For the North Koreans, to survive the escape was to eat, yes . . . but then to enter a twilight zone of existence that no person on this Earth should have to endure.

It is the Chinese and ethnic Korean Christians who greet the refugees with rice and the love of God. They open their homes at great risk, knowing that their own fate will be determined by the dangers they dare to embrace. But they take these people in willingly, sacrificially, and their faith is a testimony to the power of God in the face of abject evil.

I sat on the floor with four young boys and their plump and smiling surrogate mother, in the kitchen of her small home in a village up in the mountains. I said young boys, because they appeared to be prepubescent teenagers, but in reality were 16 and 17 years old. Their bodies were underdeveloped and malnourished due to the famine and the fact that Kim Jong Il routes humanitarian aid to the military, while starving his own people. They were told in school, incidentally, that there was no rice because the Americans had sunk the ships bringing in the food. Three of them, friends, had just recently swum across the Tumen River separating the two countries in a valiant and courageous effort to get food, and in one boy's case, take the enormous risk of bringing some of it back to his starving mother.

The boy who was planning to make that treacherous return trip was animated, smiling, filled with mission and purpose. After telling us that he had learned about God in this loving sanctuary, our interpreter asked if he would go back and declare his faith. With refreshing candor, characteristic of his colorful personality, he said softly, "I don't have that much faith yet." Another one huddled beside me, with the twisted, silent countenance only a trauma victim can display. He talked quietly about their dangerous swim across the river and how in one moment he thought he was going to die . . . How the other two boys encouraged him on and how they had persevered to the shore for freedom. Still . . . no expression . . . the voice subdued.

The woman who had taken them in was constantly moving about, touching and hugging and feeding them. She was a Christian . . . one of the band of brave souls who are risking their own lives and well being to help the people that no one wants . . . North Korean refugees. The boys were not permitted to leave the house . . . they couldn't go to school . . . work or play, because if caught, they would be sent back and summarily executed. The Chinese government doesn't want them. The South Korean government doesn't want them, and current U.S. policy severely limits sanctuary here. There is no place to go.

As we tried to leave this mountain hideaway, neighbors came out of their houses, watching, not with innocent curiosity but with the intent of spying and reporting on their rebellious neighbor. We shuddered to think of her fate as we pulled away.

The next day we ventured into a town on the border, and tried, at least, in spite of passing an unexpected prison chain gang, to enter a Chinese apartment discreetly. We quickly climbed the steps to the top floor and entered silently. We were ushered into a sort of family room where five more refugees were sitting, along with the apartment dweller, another Christian and his wife who had opened their home at great peril. Once we entered the room, the doorbell rang and an electric wave of tension surged through all of us. The man rushed to shut the door to our room, another watched nervously out the window, and we felt, in that moment, the dread fear the Chinese and North Koreans live with daily. Our hearts pounded as we realized that it was . . . a false alarm.

I proceeded to interview two of the refugees. One, a young mother, had fled across the Tumen River herself to get food for her husband and baby. She was aided once again by Christ-followers who gave her rice and a small Bible, after which she made the dangerous trip back with her treasure. She was subsequently caught and put in prison. The hatred of Christianity in North Korea is so great that if you are caught with a Bible, not only do they execute you, but your parents and children— three generations are slaughtered. She was waiting for her sentence in the prison, when she chose to jump from the top floor, an attempt to kill herself and hopefully save her family. She fell in a broken heap, and was left for dead. But she was not dead. As I sat beside her on the floor, I saw the mangled bones in her feet and legs juxtaposed to her otherwise beautiful body and face. At 24 her life was over. She had lost her husband . . . her child . . . she could not leave this apartment except in the dark of night . . . could not hold a job . . . no future . . . no hope.

Next, I turned to a 12-year-old girl hovering on a couch—another child/adult wearing the unmistakable countenance of trauma. No expression . . . just a deep, deep furrow in her brow. Words, without emotion, devoid of eye contact. She told how for the past several years she had been walking daily up into the mountains, a 10 kilometer walk one way, to spend the day picking branches off trees. She would then bundle them together, drag them back the same 10 kilometers to sell them for the American equivalent of 25 cents in the market, in order to feed her sick father and little brother. Somehow she had escaped, but in the process her little brother had disappeared. It was in reliving that moment that she broke down and could not go on with her story.

When I left that room with those people, fully comprehending the risk they had taken not only to escape but to allow me to come and hear their stories, I vowed to them on that day that they had not taken that risk in vain . . . that I would make sure their stories were told so that the world could hear.

I was a radio talk-show host at the time, confident I could go back and accomplish that. I was reporting for my new job here in Washington on October 15, but my plan was to use the two weeks I had left to expose the evil I had seen. Little did I know that my country would be attacked, leaving me and my companions stranded in Beijing, and that that would cut my remaining time on the air so short, I wouldn't have the ability to do what I had earnestly promised.

It grieved me to let them down in that way, but I couldn't see how my duties as President of Concerned Women for America would ever intersect with their need.

Leave it to the gracious God that I serve to find a way. The North Korea Freedom Coalition came about quite unexpectedly, my selection as chairman an equal surprise. But it is a surprise I welcome, and it is with the passion of one who has seen the evil of the Kim Jong Il Regime that I lead and will continue to lead this group.

I lived in Berlin, Germany, during the height of the Cold War, traveled regularly though Checkpoint Charlie into East Berlin and observed the palpable oppression of the East German people. I have been to Vietnam, China several times, and to Russia before the break up of the Soviet Union. I have tasted and smelled the evils of oppression, but I can tell you that I don't think anything matches the horror of life in North Korea. That is why I stand to speak and, if necessary, shout their cause for them today.

The North Korea Freedom Coalition is a bipartisan coalition of religious, human rights, non-governmental, Korean and American organizations whose prime purpose is to bring freedom to the North Korean people and to ensure that the human rights component of the U.S. and world policy toward North Korea receives priority attention.

We are a coalition of both the ideological left and right, ranging from The Salvation Army USA to the Religious Action Center of Reform Judaism headed by David Saperstein, because on issues of human need and desperation, we can most certainly agree.

We are strong supporters of the North Korean Freedom Act of 2003, a soon-to-be bi-partisan act that will promote human rights, democracy, and development in North Korea. The provisions contained in the act will provide safe harbor for North Korean refugees, provide ways to get information and food to those starving for both, monitor the death camps so well-detailed in David Hawk's report, and make sure that not one American dollar is spent to build another gulag.

Further, any negotiating with the North Korean regime that says "you can continue to starve and torture your people as long as you dismantle your weapons of mass destruction" is as unacceptable as it is un-American.

And while we wish no harm to our South Korean friends, we also stand to remind them that it is equally unacceptable for them to prop up a regime that is starving and torturing their relatives to the North because the consequences of saving them would be too costly.

We will encourage our government to help South Korea absorb the difficulties that may come, but only to the extent that the South ceases to aid and abet the murderous regime of the North.

Not only are we determined to get information and freedom INTO North Korea, we are determined to get the word out in the West of the brutality and starvation of the North Korean people by their "Dear Leader." We believe that by God's grace the net effect of such a movement can be much the same as the fall of both the Soviet Union and the Berlin Wall. No shots fired—just freedom imploding.

President Bush has led the way on this issue by boldly and rightly declaring North Korea part of an Axis of Evil. This is no time for the faint of heart or spineless appeasers. This is a time for Americans of all political stripes to unite for a noble purpose: To bring freedom, food and wholeness to the suffering people of North Korea.

Thank you.

Senator BROWNBACK. Thank you for that passionate, clear presentation.

Mr. Kumar, thank you very much for joining us, advocacy director for Asia and the Pacific, Amnesty International.

STATEMENT OF T. KUMAR, ADVOCACY DIRECTOR FOR ASIA AND THE PACIFIC, AMNESTY INTERNATIONAL, WASHINGTON, DC

Mr. KUMAR. Thank you very much, Mr. Chairman.

Amnesty International is extremely pleased to testify here for two important reasons. The first reason is it's a closed country. Second, the human-rights abuses that are taking place in North Korea is extremely disturbing to us.

We have been monitoring human rights around the world for more than 40 years. Our only job is monitoring human rights, not to take into consideration any other issues. First, I will list what abuses we have encountered there, which we have seen there. Second, I will go into details about what we feel is the best approach to deal with the abuses that are taking place.

As I mentioned to you earlier, Mr. Chairman, this is a closed country. So the information that we get has to be extremely scrutinized and be verified. But despite these difficulties, we were able to come up with some excellent reporting of what's happening there.

I think we are the only human-rights organization which was allowed to go to North Korea. We visited North Korea in 1995. But since we were not able to get free access to persons in other places, we came out and issued a very harsh statement in 1995.

The issues that we are concerned are public executions, where people have been gathered around grounds and people have been executed for various crimes, including people who have been sent back from China. Some of them have been executed. Torture resulting in death, inhumane prison conditions, and large-scale abuses and other abuses like torture, as I mentioned earlier.

I would like to bring your attention to one issue that's disturbing us for the last 3 or 4 years.

That's the issue of starvation and death.

In mid 1990s, North Korea experienced famine and, as a result of famine, starvation due to natural disasters and economic mismanagement. The result of is, this is not our figure, it's the U.N. figure, is that 2 million people have died because of that famine and mismanagement of economic resources. Almost 40 percent of the children are chronically malnourished.

Senator BROWNBACK. Currently?

Mr. KUMAR. They are extremely chronically malnourished.

Senator BROWNBACK. But that's a current number?

Mr. KUMAR. Yes, that's the number—that's a U.N. figure.

41

Almost half the population—that is 13 million—are also malnourished. And we are extremely fearful that any food embargoes that's being enforced, for whatever reason, can hurt the most vulnerable, like the children, elderly, pregnant women, nursing women, and the elderly. So we appeal to you, Mr. Chairman, please d-link any food embargoes when you consider any political consideration toward North Korea. We discussed this pretty much intensely internally as an organization, and we came up with the decision that our responsibility and the world's responsibility is to the people of North Korea. We should separate North Korean people from the regime. So we can't afford to have another 2 million perish because of famine there because we may be angry with the regime there. We can't allow children who are born because of famine, and then going through severe physical and mental problems when they are growing up. So that's our plea to you, Mr. Chairman.

And how best to achieve transparency and to deal with North Korea is something—we thought the U.N. is the best method. Even though North Koreans invited us in 1995, they are extremely closed and extremely nervous about outsiders interfering into their so-called internal affairs. They have ratified four major U.N. conventions—civil and political rights, economic and social rights, the children's rights. So they have an obligation and duty to invite special rapporteurs to visit these—from these conventions to visit North Korea to investigate impartially. We will urge the administration and you to take the leadership in exerting pressure through the U.N. so that these people can—these special rapporteurs can make an impartial intervention in North Korea and find out what's happening there. That will be our recommendation, in terms of seeing what's happening inside in this closed country.

In closing, Mr. Chairman, I would like to appeal to you again. We are extremely worried about the people of North Korea. We should never punish average citizens for somebody else's mistake. Let U.S. and other countries stand up and continue the food aid as they are giving now.

Thank you very much.

[The prepared statement of Mr. Kumar follows:]

PREPARED STATEMENT OF T. KUMAR, ADVOCACY DIRECTOR FOR ASIA AND THE PACIFIC, AMNESTY INTERNATIONAL USA

Thank you Mr. Chairman and distinguished members of this committee. Amnesty International is pleased to testify at this important hearing. The human rights situation in North Korea has been a consistent and grave concern to Amnesty International. We last visited the country in 1995 but were not allowed to undertake independent monitoring. Since that time, numerous attempts to enter the country to assess the human rights situation have been denied by the North Korean authorities. Despite the North Korean government's lack of cooperation, we have received numerous credible reports of grave abuses.

Amnesty International's long-standing concerns about human rights violations in North Korea include the use of torture, the death penalty, arbitrary detention and imprisonment, inhumane prison conditions and the near-total suppression of fundamental freedoms, including freedom of expression, religion, and movement.

In recent years, many human rights abuses in North Korea have been linked directly or indirectly to the famine and acute food shortages, which have affected the country since the mid-1990s. The famine and persistent acute food shortages have led to widespread malnutrition among the population and to the movement of hundreds of thousands of people in search of food—some across the border with China—

many have become the victims of human rights violations as a result of their search for food and survival.

In this context, Amnesty International believes that guaranteeing equitable distribution of food to all individuals in North Korea without discrimination is a key priority which the North Korean government must address urgently, in line with its international obligations, with appropriate assistance from the international community. The United States Government can play a leading role in helping to ensure that thousands of innocent civilians are spared the horrors of malnutrition and deaths due to hunger.

UNITED NATIONS HUMAN RIGHTS COMMISSION

In a resolution on North Korea passed at the 58th session of the UN Commission on Human Rights in April 2003, the Commission expressing the Commission's deep concern about reports of systemic, widespread and grave violations of human rights in North Korea, including "torture, public executions, and imposition of the death penalty for political reasons."

In the resolution, the Commission also expressed concern at "the existence of a large number of prison camps, the extensive use of forced labour, and the lack of respect for the rights of persons deprived of their liberty." Other areas of concern included reports of "all-pervasive and severe restrictions on the freedoms of thought, conscience, religion, opinion and expression, peaceful assembly and association and on access of everyone to information, and limitations imposed on every person who wishes to move freely within the country and travel abroad."

The resolution also called on Pyongyang to implement "its obligations under the International Covenant on Economic, Social and Cultural Rights, in particular concerning the right of everyone to be free from hunger." The resolution also requested "the international community to continue to urge that humanitarian assistance, especially food aid, destined for the people of the Democratic People's Republic of Korea, be distributed in accordance with humanitarian principles and to ensure also the respect of the fundamental principles of asylum."

RESTRICTIONS ON ACCESS

There is little detailed information on the extent of human rights violations in North Korea due to the restrictions on access to the country for independent human rights monitors. Information and access to the country remain tightly controlled, hampering the investigation of the human rights situation on the ground. However, reports from a variety of sources suggest a pattern of serious human rights violations, such as those described below.

EXECUTIONS

Amnesty International has received reports of public executions carried out at places where large crowds gather. These executions are announced in advance to encourage attendance by schools, enterprises, and farms. Some prisoners have reportedly been executed in front of their families. Executions are carried out by hanging or firing-squad.

FREEDOM OF EXPRESSION AND RELIGION

Opposition of any kind is not tolerated. According to reports, any person who expresses an opinion contrary to the position of the ruling party faces severe punishment, as does their family in many cases. The domestic news media is strictly censored and access to international media broadcasts is restricted. Any unauthorized assembly or association is regarded as a "collective disturbance", liable to punishment.

Religious freedom, although guaranteed by the constitution, is in practice sharply curtailed. There are reports of severe repression of people involved in public and private religious activities through imprisonment, torture and executions. Many Christians are reportedly being held in labor camps.

TORTURE AND ILL-TREATMENT

Reports from a variety of sources suggest that torture and ill-treatment are widespread in prisons and labor camps, as well as in detention centers where North Koreans who have been forcibly returned from China are held for interrogation pending transfer to other places. Conditions in prisons and labor camps are reported to be extremely harsh. Inmates are made to work from early morning until late at night in farms or factories, and minor infractions of rules can be met with severe

43

beatings. According to some reports, however, more deaths are caused by lack of food, harsh conditions and lack of medical care than by torture or ill-treatment.

FREEDOM FROM HUNGER AND MALNUTRITION

North Korea continues to rely on international aid to feed its population, but many people in the country are suffering from hunger and malnutrition. According to a study published last year by the Food and Agricultural Organization of the United Nations (FAO), 13 million people in North Korea—over half of the population—suffered from malnutrition. Aid agencies have estimated that up to two million people have died since the mid-1990s as a result of acute food shortages caused by natural disasters and economic mismanagement. Several million children suffer from chronic malnutrition, impairing their physical and mental development. Many people in the country also lack adequate medical care due to lack of medical personnel and supplies.

According to a special report by the FAO and the World Food Program (WFP) on October 30, 2003, despite improved harvests, North Korea will have another substantial food deficit in 2004. A combination of "insufficient domestic production, the narrow and inadequate diet of much of the population and growing disparities in access to food as the purchasing power of many household declines" has meant that about 6.5 million North Koreans will require assistance next year.

The situation remains "especially precarious" for young children, pregnant and nursing women and elderly people. Malnutrition rates remain "alarmingly high", as four out of ten young children suffer from chronic malnutrition, or stunting, according to a survey conducted in October 2002 by the UNICEF and the WFP. According to FAO and the WFP, "Continued, targeted food aid interventions are essential to prevent a slippage back towards previous, higher levels of malnutrition."

An economic policy adjustment process initiated by the North Korean government in July 2002 has led to a further decrease in the already inadequate purchasing power of many urban households. The new report cites government authorities who state that rations from the Public Distribution System (PDS)—the primary source of food for 70 percent of the population living in urban areas—are set to decline to no more than 300 grams per person per day in 2004, from 319 grams this year. Although the PDS rations are very low, industrial workers and elderly people now spend more than half of their income on these rations alone. They are unable to purchase staples such as rice and maize from private markets, where prices are as much as 3.5 times higher, let alone more nutritious foods.

Freedom from hunger and malnutrition and the right to food are fundamental rights guaranteed in the International Covenant on Economic, Social and Cultural Rights (ICESCR), to which North Korea is a State Party. The provision of food where humanitarian assistance is needed is both a joint and individual responsibility. The expert Committee set up to monitor the Covenant has concluded that all State Parties, individually and through international cooperation, are under an obligation to ensure "an equitable distribution of world food supplies in relation to need".

North Korea must ensure that international food aid and other food supplies are distributed equitably to all among its population, without discrimination. If its population is in need of food supplies that it cannot provide, the government must seek outside assistance, and must refrain from using food as a negotiating issue.

Amnesty International wrote to President Bush in July 2003 commending the Administration's announcement that the US Government would refrain from using food as an instrument of political and economic pressure and seeking further assurances that this will remain US policy. States such as the USA, which are in a position to help the North Korean population, must provide the necessary food aid, without tying this to particular political goals. The US government responded in August, assuring that the policy of the United States is to provide emergency food aid based on humanitarian considerations without regard to political, military or economic issues; however, there has been a decline in food aid to North Korea in recent years. This trend has continued despite concerns from the WFP and other humanitarian agencies of substantial shortfalls in food aid and serious levels of chronic malnutrition among vulnerable sections of the population.

Should the US, which has been a leading donor of humanitarian food aid to North Korea in the past, impose food embargoes or reductions in food aid to North Korea, it is the ordinary North Korean people who would suffer more. The worsening food shortage would also lead to worsening conditions for already vulnerable sectors of the North Korean population, such as children, women and elderly people. As a prominent aid donor stated, "Withholding aid would not only be morally wrong, it would also not solve any problems. Closing the door now means much greater dif-

44

ficulty in reopening the future—and with an open door comes the possibility of the same level of communication, or of gradually developing an even better level (of communication)." Food should not be used as an instrument of political and economic pressure and must be the subject of embargoes.

NORTH KOREAN ASYLUM SEEKERS IN CHINA

In the face of serious food shortages and political repression, thousands of North Koreans have fled across the border to China where many live in fear of arrest and possible repatriation. The Chinese authorities claim that all North Koreans who illegally come to China are economic migrants, and have consistently denied them access to any refugee determination procedure, in violation of China's obligations under the 1951 Refugee Convention and despite evidence that many among them have genuine claims to asylum.

Their desperate plight has been brought into sharp focus by a series of diplomatic incidents in which over 100 North Koreans have entered foreign diplomatic facilities in several Chinese cities in an attempt to claim asylum. China has responded to these incidents by stepping up its crackdown on North Koreans, particularly in the provinces of Liaoning and Jilin which border North Korea. Hundreds, possibly thousands, of North Koreans have been detained and forcibly returned across the border where they meet an uncertain fate. Amnesty International fears that they could be subjected to serious human rights violations as discussed below, including arbitrary detention, torture or even summary execution.

The renewed crackdown in northeast China has also extended to people suspected of helping North Koreans, including members of foreign aid and religious organizations and ethnic Korean Chinese nationals living in the border area, many of whom have been detained for interrogation. In December 2001, a South Korean pastor, Chun Ki-won, and his assistant, Jin Qilong, an ethnic Korean Chinese national, were arrested in Hulunbeier City in China's Inner Mongolia Autonomous Region while leading a group of 13 North Koreans through northeast China towards the neighboring state of Mongolia. On March 3, 2002, Chun Ki-won and Jin Qilong were charged with "organizing other people to illegally cross the national border". They were tried by the Hulunbeier Municipal People's Court in Inner Mongolia in July, found guilty and sentenced to pay fines of 50,000 and 20,000 Yuan respectively (US$6,000/US$2,400). They were subsequently released, and Chun Ki-won was deported to South Korea on August 22, 2002.

The 13 North Koreans were detained in Manzhouli Prison in Inner Mongolia. Three of them, including a newly-born baby, were reportedly returned to North Korea in late January or early February 2002, but there were no further details about their status or whereabouts. The others, including four children, were reported to have been moved from Manzhouli Prison in July 2002, but their current whereabouts remain unknown.

More recently, five men were arrested on January 18, 2003 in Yantai for helping North Koreans, and were sentenced on May 22, 2003. They include a South Korean journalist, Seok Jae-hyun, who was sentenced to two years and a fine of 5,000 Yuan and another South Korean national, Choi Yong-hun, who was sentenced to five years and fined 30,000 Yuan.

Despite the uncertain fate that awaits them, many North Koreans continue to cross the border into China. Some have sought asylum in diplomatic compounds and foreign schools in China and have been allowed to leave, traveling to South Korea via third countries. Hundreds of others have been reportedly apprehended in northeast China and forcibly returned to North Korea.

Those forcibly returned are held for interrogation in detention centers or police stations operated by North Korean security agencies. Depending on who they are and the result of interrogation, they may be sent back to detention centers or prisons in their home province, or to labor camps for up to six months. A few such returnees, particularly former officials or those found with religious literature, are assigned long terms of imprisonment with hard labor or in some cases face execution. Those sent back to their home province are ostracized within their community and subjected to surveillance. Many flee the country again. Some have fled and been returned several times, reportedly facing increasingly severe punishments with each failed escape attempt.

WHAT CAN BE DONE?

Mr. Chairman, given the closed nature of North Korea and continued reports of numerous human rights abuses, it is imperative that the international community find the best way to encourage increased transparency in the country. We are not aware of any independent functioning civil society or non-governmental organizations in North Korea.

The international community should focus on persuading North Korea to invite United Nations human rights experts as a first step. Transparency in a closed country environment like North Korea, especially with respect to its prisons and detention centers, is more likely to be achieved in a gradual, step-by-step manner. Because North Korea is a member of the United Nations, it may be more inclined to allow access to the United Nations than any other organization. Countries like South Korea, China, Japan, EU member countries and Russia could be helpful allies in this endeavor.

RECOMMENDATIONS TO THE BUSH ADMINISTRATION

- Engage diplomatically with North Korean government authorities;
- Initiate confidence-building measures such as continuation of food aid without conditionality and avoid food sanctions;
- Urge North Korea to grant unimpeded access to international human rights organizations;
- Urge North Korea to allow UN human rights monitors access to prisons and detention facilities;
- Urge North Korea to grant unimpeded access to Special Rapporteurs and thematic experts under the United Nations conventions to which North Korea is a state party, such as the International Convention on Civil and Political Rights (ICCPR); International Convention on Economic, Social and Cultural Rights (ICESCR); Convention on the Rights of the Child (CRC); and Convention on the Elimination of all forms of Discrimination against Women (CEDAW);
- Urge the North Korean government to implement the recommendations of the Committee on Human Rights and the Committee on the Rights of the Child, which were issued in response to the reports on treaty compliance submitted by North Korea;
- Urge the North Korean government to grant access to the Special Rapporteur on Food to make visits to prisons and detention centers where there have been reports of deaths due to malnutrition;
- Urge the North Korean government to invite experts from the Committee on the Rights of the Child and thematic experts and rapporteurs under CEDAW, as children and pregnant and nursing women are identified by UN agencies as vulnerable groups badly affected by the food shortages in North Korea. These experts should be granted unimpeded access to prisons or detention centers for juvenile detainees and women detainees;
- Urge the North Korean government to grant access to and cooperate without restriction/reservation with thematic procedures of the Commission on Human Rights relevant to the situation of North Korea: the Special Rapporteur on Torture, the Special Rapporteur on Religious Intolerance, the Working Group on Arbitrary Detention, as well as the Working Group on Enforced or Involuntary Disappearances; encourage North Korean government to report regularly to the relevant treaty bodies, ratify more UN Conventions, including the Convention against Torture and other Cruel, Inhuman or Degrading Treatment or Punishment;
- Urge North Korea to review existing legislation to ensure it conforms with international human rights standards and introduce safeguards to provide citizens with protections and remedies against human rights violations;
- Prohibit the use of slave, forced, or prison labor in any investment in extraction or production enterprises.

RECOMMENDATIONS TO THE CHINESE GOVERNMENT

- Allow the United Nations High Commissioner for Refugees (UNHCR) access to North Korean refugees in China;
- Stop repatriating North Korean refugees.

RECOMMENDATIONS TO THE NORTH KOREAN GOVERNMENT

Amnesty International has repeatedly called on the North Korean government to take measures to increase respect for human rights in the country, including to:

- Abide by the principles laid out in the international human rights treaties it has ratified—such as the International Covenant on Civil and Political Rights and the International Covenant on Economic, Social and Cultural Rights—and incorporate these principles into domestic law;

- Abolish the death penalty;
- Release all who are detained or imprisoned for the peaceful exercise of their human rights;
- Guarantee freedom of expression, religion, movement for all North Koreans;
- Ensure the right to freedom from hunger and malnutrition without discrimination;
- Review and revise existing legislation to ensure it conforms with international human rights standards and introduce safeguards to provide citizens with protections and remedies against human rights violations; and
- Grant unimpeded access to international human rights organizations and other independent human rights monitors;
- Invite the UN human rights mechanisms to visit North Korea, in particular to grant unimpeded access to Special Rapporteurs and thematic experts under the United Nations conventions to which North Korea is a state party, such as the International Convention on Civil and Political Rights (ICCPR), International Convention on Economic, Social and Cultural Rights (ICESCR), Convention on the Rights of the Child (CRC), and Convention on the Elimination of all forms of Discrimination against Women (CEDAW);
- Implement the recommendations of the Committee on Human Rights and the Committee on the Rights of the Child, which were issued in response to North Korea's treaty compliance report;
- Invite the Special Rapporteur on Food to visit prisons and detention centers where there have been reports of deaths due to malnutrition;
- Invite experts from the Committee on the Rights of the Child and thematic experts and rapporteurs under CEDAW, to examine conditions generally and also focus on children and pregnant and nursing women who have been identified by UN agencies as vulnerable groups badly affected by the food shortages. In addition, provide these experts with unimpeded access to prisons or detention centers for juvenile detainees and women detainees;
- Grant access to and cooperate without restriction or reservation with the thematic procedures of the Commission on Human Rights, such as the Special Rapporteur on Torture, the Special Rapporteur on Religious Intolerance, the Working Group on Arbitrary Detention, as well as the Working Group on Enforced or Involuntary Disappearances;
- Submit reports regularly to the relevant UN treaty bodies of experts and ratify additional human rights related UN conventions, including the Convention against Torture and other Cruel, Inhuman or Degrading Treatment or Punishment.

Thank you.

Senator BROWNBACK. Thank you very much, Mr. Kumar.

Mr. Charny. Tell me if I'm getting that—pronounce it for me.

Mr. CHARNY. Charny.

Senator BROWNBACK. Charny, excuse me. Thank you very much for being here with us today.

STATEMENT OF JOEL R. CHARNY, VICE PRESIDENT FOR POLICY, REFUGEES INTERNATIONAL, WASHINGTON, DC

Mr. CHARNY. Thank you. And, Senator Brownback, I'd especially like to thank you for organizing this hearing on humanitarian and human-rights issues related to North Korea, and for your overall commitment to human rights in that country.

We believe precisely that focus on the nuclear issue, as critical as that issue is to the security of the United States and East Asia, has deflected attention from the terrible humanitarian situation of the North Korean people. And RI appreciates the consistent efforts of the members of this committee to bring attention to the humanitarian and human-rights aspects of the North Korea problem.

I will present a very brief summary of our findings and recommendations, while requesting that my full written testimony be entered into the record.

Senator BROWNBACK. Without objection.

Mr. CHARNY. My testimony is based on a visit to one province in China, in June of this year, interviewing 38 North Korean refugees, ranging in age from 13 to 51. And like Ms. Rios, I had similar experiences in just the emotional content of the testimony that we are hearing, people speaking very matter-of-fact about the death of relatives, about the starvation and suffering that they had faced in North Korea, about arrest and deportation in China, return to North Korea, and facing difficult conditions again. And it was a one-week trip. We only spoke to 38 people, but I think it was one of the most intense experiences I've ever been through as an advocate for Refugees International.

My analogy is to Cambodia, under the Khmer Rouge, a situation that I'm familiar with from long work on Cambodia.

I don't think any other country in the world, with the possible exception of Pol Pot's Cambodia, has created such a controlled society where there's just—there's no air, there's no space, there's truly no freedom for people to act and to be human beings.

Our first interview was with a man who had crossed 3 days before, and we asked him what his reaction was to China. And he hesitated for a moment, and then he just broke into tears, and he had to leave the room, and when he returned, he basically said, you just have to understand how shocking it is "to see the freedom in China"—freedom in China, put that in perspective—the "immense wealth"—again, put that in perspective—that the North Koreans find in China just completely shatters their world.

Now, to summarize our findings, credible local sources that monitor the border place the number of North Koreans in China between 60,000 and 100,000. Now, I know that estimate is low, but I have full confidence in this NGO and the networks that they're a part of. They monitor the border very closely, and I think we need to start using maybe more realistic estimates for the numbers of North Koreans in China today.

The primary motivation of North Korean refugees to cross the border is to ensure their survival, and I think I want to insist on that terminology. "Economic reasons" somehow imply that, they're crossing China to become businessmen or, to seek employment in a factory. Fundamentally, it's about survival.

There's a great deal of movement back and forth across the border, movement which is tolerated by the North Korean and Chinese border guards when they believe it really is for survival reasons.

Fifty percent of the refugees that I interviewed had been arrested and deported at least once. The treatment of the refugees upon being deported was consistent—2 months of captivity in a labor training center, where they endure harsh labor and starvation rations, as David Hawk details in his report. This treatment, coupled with the political manipulation of food rations and employment opportunities inside North Korea, constitutes the case for considering the North Koreans in China deserving of refugee status. They should not be considered economic migrants. That's clear.

Trafficking of women is a serious problem, but based on my 1 week in China, it's impossible to give a precise estimate of its scope. Korean women do cross with the deliberate intention of marrying Korean Chinese men as a survival strategy, and I think we need to recognize that.

The problem is that they're exceedingly vulnerable to being captured and sold to Chinese husbands or to bar and brothel owners well outside the border region. But we only interviewed one woman, who had, indeed, been sent from Jilin to southern China, who had managed to escape and to return to that area. So, again, in a short period of time, it's just impossible to estimate the number of women who might be trapped in trafficking networks.

Now, I want to mention the following strategies for protection and recommendations as to how to deal with the North Korean situation in China.

First, the border with China is the lifeline for North Koreans, and therein lies the dilemma. Providing real protection while avoiding counterproductive provocations of the Chinese Government is a very difficult challenge. We recommend—it's obvious, David Hawk said the same—that China stop arresting and deporting law-abiding North Korean refugees. Now, Senator, as you well know, China has signed the 1951 convention and 1967 protocol related to the status of refugees, and in this context, to add insult to injury, is a member of the UNHCR Executive Committee, yet still they will not allow the Office of the U.N. High Commissioner for Refugees access to the border region. And I tend to agree with UNHCR here that it's not about the agreement between the Government of China and UNHCR, which is just a technical agreement relating to their representation in Beijing. What's fundamental is that China's a signatory to the Refugee Convention and, further, is a member of the UNHCR Executive Committee. The United States has got to work that issue in the UNHCR Executive Committee.

Senator BROWNBACK. Let me stop you just there, if I could, Mr. Charny. How can we do that more effectively?

Because I just think this is ridiculous, that they would be on the Executive Committee. They've got one of the worst human-rights abuse situations right on their border.

Everybody outside of the area is documenting this. We have photos of this. How do we get the Chinese to act?

Mr. CHARNY. Well, as you well know, getting China to move on any human-rights issue is not easy. We've spoken to a high official in the Bureau of Population Refugees and Migration and also people in Democracy, Human Rights, and Labor, and they do assure us, these officials assure us, that this situation is on the agenda in the bilateral dialog between the United States and China on human-rights issues.

My hesitation or my doubt is whether this is really rising to the level that it should. In other words, let's get this up higher on the agenda in our discussions with the Chinese. And then I think the Executive Committee of UNHCR meets periodically. There is an opportunity for the United States to either make private contact with the Chinese in the context of the Executive Committee—that probably wouldn't work. At some point, I think we need to go public. UNHCR is saying, "there's little we can do without real political support." And the United States is a global leader on human-rights issues. We give more money to UNHCR probably than any government in the world. I think we have leverage and an opportunity to raise this publicly within the framework of the UNHCR Executive Committee. So it's about a more public posture on this issue, recognizing that China often reacts negatively to public pressure. But, again, the very idea that they're on the Executive Committee, I think, gives us the opening to work this issue in a public forum.

That's my reaction. It's not an easy issue to deal with, I admit.

Now, resettlement is a possible protection strategy, but, again, we're stuck with the Chinese being the easiest country of first asylum, and they would have to be convinced to make resettlement a legal process. The problem with resettlement right now is, it's a clandestine process that involves either embassy seizures or the underground railroad to South Korea or, as David Hawk alluded to earlier, an underground railroad that takes North Koreans on an unimaginable journey through southern China, into Vietnam, across Cambodia, sometimes down through Laos to Thailand. I can't imagine making that journey as a North Korean refugee.

Again, part of our effort with China should be to get them to agree to grant access—and we could limit the numbers at the outset—but we need access to North Koreans so that we can resettle North Koreans legally, openly, transparently. You know, the underground railroad is amazing, but the numbers are too small. It doesn't really make enough of a difference at this stage.

Now, the South Korean reluctance was something I knew little about until I went to Seoul in June, and, frankly, I was surprised at the limited numbers of North Koreans that are accepted in South Korea for resettlement and the evident ambivalence of the South Koreans about taking more. Again, can we work this issue with the South Koreans to get them to raise their numbers from a thousand, which I think is minimal, up to more like 2,000, 3,000, or 5,000 a year, numbers I think would be reasonable under the circumstances.

Now, the United States has previous experience in resettling isolated and difficult-to-assimilate populations, such as the Hmong, from Laos. So I think we could bring that experience to bear, accept North Koreans for resettlement, and also provide technical training and support to South Korean Government agencies and NGOs involved in resettlement.

And then, finally, I've referred to the underground railway. I think American Embassy staff in Southeast Asian countries should obviously be on the lookout for North Korea asylum-seekers, and be prepared to consider them for possible resettlement in the United States.

Thank you.

[The prepared statement of Mr. Charny follows:]

PREPARED STATEMENT OF JOEL R. CHARNY, VICE PRESIDENT FOR POLICY, REFUGEES INTERNATIONAL, WASHINGTON, DC

I would like to thank Senator Richard G. Lugar, Chairman of the Senate Committee on Foreign Relations, and Senator Sam Brownback, Chairman of the East Asia Subcommittee, for organizing this hearing on humanitarian and human rights issues related to North Korea and for inviting me to testify on behalf of Refugees International. RI believes that the focus on the nuclear issue, as critical as that issue is to the security of the United States and East Asia, has deflected attention from the terrible humanitarian situation of the North Korean people. RI appreciates the consistent efforts of the members of this Committee to bring attention to the humanitarian and human rights aspects of the North Korea problem.

In June I spent one week with a colleague in Jilin province in China interviewing North Korean refugees. They live a precarious and clandestine existence as illegal migrants in Jilin, which is the home of some one million Chinese of Korean ethnicity. Through contacts with networks of non-governmental organizations, largely affiliated with local pastors supported by donations from Christian communities in South Korea and the United States, the RI team conducted interviews of 38 North Koreans, ranging in age from 13 to 51. This experience, as limited as it was, constitutes, to our knowledge, the most extensive interviewing of North Korean refugees in China by an American organization in 2003.

The estimates of the number of North Koreans in China vary widely—from under 100,000 to as high as 300,000. The organizations that hosted the RI visit monitor border crossings on a daily basis and through their service programs keep a close eye on the total number of North Koreans needing support at any given time. They incline towards the lower estimate, and having seen first hand the care with which they approach the question of numbers, RI accepts their estimate of 60-100,000 North Koreans presently in northeast China.

The primary motivation of the North Koreans crossing into China is either to find a better life in China or to access food and other basic supplies to bring back to their families in North Korea. Among the 38 people that RI interviewed, no one had experienced direct persecution for her or his political beliefs or religious affiliation prior to crossing the border for the first time. The Chinese government argues, therefore, that the Koreans are economic migrants rather than refugees, and should be treated the same way that the U.S. treats illegal migrants from Mexico or Haiti.

From a refugee rights perspective, China's reasoning is flawed. The fundamental problem is that North Koreans are subject to special persecution upon being deported from China, with the minimum period of detention in "labor training centers," which are tantamount to prisons, being two months. Second, everyone in North Korea is divided into political classes, with less privileged people, who constitute the majority with suspect revolutionary credentials, receiving lower rations and less access to full employment. The deprivation that North Koreans are fleeing cannot be isolated from the system of political oppression that epitomizes the North Korean regime. These factors taken together give North Koreans a strong case for being considered refugees in their country of first asylum.

THE CURRENT SITUATION FOR NORTH KOREAN REFUGEES IN CHINA

The experience of conducting 38 interviews of North Korean refugees over the space of a week was harrowing. While the demeanor of the refugees ranged from a matter-of-fact passivity to emotional fragility to defiance, the stories that they told were consistent in their grim portrayal of life in North Korea and the losses that they had suffered, especially during the famine period, but in some cases more recently. Most of the refugees that RI interviewed were originally from areas in the far north and east of the country, regions that had been denied international food aid during the famine as described in USAID Administrator Andrew Natsios' book, The Great North Korea Famine. Approximately half of the refugees had lost at least one relative to starvation or disease and an equal portion had been arrested in China and deported at least once. The following account illustrates what North Korean refugees go through:

We first came to China in 1997. We have been arrested and deported a total of three times. In April 2002 my husband, my son, and I were arrested. My daughter happened to be out at the time. We were taken to the border crossing point at Tumen and handed to the North Korean security guards. We first went to the county labor training center, then to the local one in our home town. We worked on construction and road building projects, and were provided only with bad corn and corn porridge for food.

In June 2002 my husband and I returned to China. My son was delivered to the border by another person. We returned to where we were staying in China and found our daughter.

We were arrested again in September 2002. This time it was the whole family. In October my daughter and I returned to China, but my husband and son stayed in North Korea. In February they tried to come, but they were arrested in North Korea. My son was sent to an orphanage this time, and my husband to a labor training center. He got sick there, was released, and died three days after his release. My son tried three times to escape from the orphanage and return to China, but each time he was caught and returned. Finally, he was able to escape and re-join us in China in March.

In April my daughter and I were arrested again and deported. On this return I learned that my husband had died. My son had not known. We were again put in the local labor training center. I wanted to see the grave of my husband, so the guards allowed me and my daughter to leave. We then escaped again and returned to China.

The testimony of recent arrivals, nine of whom had come to China this year and three of whom had crossed into China within a week of our meeting, belied the reports that the North Korean economy has been improving in response to the limited economic reforms initiated in July 2002. In separate interviews, the recent arrivals, who were largely from North Hamyung, reputedly one of the poorest provinces in North Korea, consistently stated that the public distribution system, which prior to 1994 assured the availability of basic food for the population, had completely collapsed. The economic reform program has resulted in rampant inflation. The price of rice and other basic commodities has skyrocketed, while wages—for coal miners, for example—have not kept pace. Children receive no food distributions at school, and many schools have stopped functioning while teachers and students search for means to survive.

What is especially shattering for North Koreans is the contrast between their life of misery and the life lived by Chinese of Korean ethnicity across the narrow border. The Tumen River, which marks the northernmost part of the border between North Korea and China, is no wider than 100 yards and shallow enough to walk across in certain spots in summer. Yet it marks an Amazonian divide in living standards and economic freedom. When RI asked a 35-year-old North Korean man who had arrived in China just three days earlier his initial impression of China, his eyes welled up. He bowed his head and he began sobbing. The stunning contrast between his life of fear and deprivation in North Korea and the relative wealth he found on the other bank of the Tumen River was shattering. Even refugees who had been in China longer could not help expressing their gratitude and amazement that in China they ate rice three times a day.

The constant threat of arrest and deportation, however, means that China is far from a paradise for North Koreans. Men have a difficult time finding sanctuary in China because staying at home is not an option and moving around Yanji city or rural areas to find day labor exposes them to police searches. The few long-staying male refugees who RI interviewed were established in a safe house deep in the countryside with access to agricultural plots in the surrounding forest. Otherwise, men tend to cross the border, hook up quickly with the refugee support organizations, access food and other supplies, and then return to their homes in North Korea. RI's impression based on very limited data is that this back and forth movement, when the motivation is clearly to obtain emergency rations, is tolerated by the North Korean and Chinese border guards.

One protection strategy available to women is trying to find a Korean-Chinese husband. The problem is that these women are vulnerable to unscrupulous traffickers who pose as honest brokers for Chinese men. RI was unable to define the scope of this problem, but anecdotal evidence suggests that the trafficking of North Korean women is widespread. Women, some of whom have a husband and children in North Korea, willingly offer themselves to gangs along the border who sell them to Chinese men. These women see this as their only option for survival. RI interviewed several women who, knowing that they were going to be sold, escaped from the traffickers once in China. Other North Korean women are successful in finding a Korean-Chinese husband and achieve a measure of stability in their lives. Probably the two happiest refugees that we spoke to during our week in China were two women who were part of stable marriages. These women, however, like all North Koreans, are unable to obtain legal residency in China. If the couple has children born in China, the children are stateless. North Korean children in China are not able to get a formal education.

The accounts of the treatment of refugees upon arrest and deportation were remarkably consistent across the range of individuals that RI interviewed. Refugees arrested in Yanji and surrounding areas in Yangbian were handed to the North Korean authorities at the border crossing point at Tumen. They were then transported to "labor training centers" in their village or town of origin in North Korea. The length of detention in these centers was consistently two months. Conditions in the centers were terrible. The deported refugees experienced hard labor on construction projects or in the fields, with very limited rations. A thin porridge made from the remnants of milled corn was the most common food. Medical care was completely unavailable. Indeed, RI was struck by several accounts indicating that severely ill detainees were released rather than cared for, presumably so they would die outside the center, freeing the guards from any responsibility for burial.

The North Koreans consider meeting with foreigners, especially with South Koreans to arrange emigration to South Korea, and adopting Christianity with the intention of propagating the faith inside North Korea to be serious crimes. According to several refugees, the punishment for deported refugees suspected of either act is life imprisonment in a maximum security prison camp or execution. For obvious reasons, RI was not able to interview anyone who had been arrested for these "crimes."

STRATEGIES FOR PROTECTING NORTH KOREAN REFUGEES

Refugees International recognizes that horrendous oppression and economic mismanagement inside North Korea are responsible for the flow of people seeking assistance and protection in China and elsewhere in Asia. In this sense, only fundamental change inside North Korea will staunch the flow of refugees and bring freedom and economic security to the North Korean population. Analyzing ways to bring about the necessary changes with the least possible suffering, however, lies outside the scope of RI's expertise. I will therefore limit my remarks to near-term protection strategies in the context of the current political situation.

The border with China is the lifeline for North Koreans in desperate condition, and therein lies the dilemma for those seeking to provide sustenance and protection for them. Any strategy for protecting North Korean refugees must be carried out in such a way that the approach does not result in steps that restrict access to supplies and security, or that lead to further arrests and crackdowns. Providing real protection while avoiding counterproductive provocations of the Chinese government is a difficult challenge.

Despite this challenge, and the proven difficulties of changing the approach of the People's Republic of China on any human right issue, Refugees International believes that a practical, near-term protection strategy must first and foremost seek to establish greater security for North Koreans in Jilin province in China. The refugees that RI interviewed either expressed an intention to return to their families in North Korea after recuperating and obtaining basic supplies or to stay and try to make their way in China. The Chinese government has designated Yangbian as a Korean autonomous region; in consequence government officials are of Korean ethnicity and Korean is the official language of government affairs and commerce, along with Mandarin. Thus, North Korean refugees have cultural and linguistic affinity with Chinese in this region. Local officials try to avoid harassing the refugees and the periodic waves of arrests and deportations, according to local sources, are the consequence of orders from the national authorities in Beijing. The economy in the border area is vibrant, due in part to South Korean investment, but living in the regional capital, Yanji, or in smaller towns does not pose the immense problems of cultural adaptation that North Koreans have faced in the South.

RI believes that the first step towards providing protection for North Korean refugees in China is for the Chinese government to stop arresting and deporting law abiding North Koreans who have found a home across the border. Given the factors favoring assimilation, and the healthy economy in Yangbian, this step should pose no immediate security or other threat to China. The UN High Commissioner for Refugees, Ruud Lubbers, claimed in June that Chinese officials had informed him that they would stop arresting and deporting North Koreans. China immediately denied any change in policy. But quiet implementation of this approach would provide greater security to North Koreans while keeping the border open to the back and forth movement of people and goods that is a lifeline for poor people in the border provinces of North Korea. Given the available options, this best combines care for North Korean refugees with respect for the legitimate political and economic security needs of the Chinese government.

Merely stopping the arrest and deportation of North Koreans, however, falls well short of China's obligations under the 1951 Convention and 1967 Protocol Related to the Status of Refugees, to which it is a signatory. Further, China is on the Executive Committee of the Office of the UN High Commissioner for Refugees (UNHCR). Yet China not only refuses to grant refugee status to worthy North Korean asylum seekers, but prevents the Beijing-based staff of UNHCR from traveling to Yangbian to assess the situation.

RI has called for UNHCR to engage proactively with the Chinese government to seek permission to visit Yangbian and eventually to establish an office in the region to monitor the status of North Koreans in China and to provide protection and assistance as needed. UNHCR's profile on this issue has been too low, considering the numbers of North Koreans in China and China's importance to UNHCR and the international community.

At the same time, RI recognizes that UNHCR's real leverage with the Chinese government on this issue is minimal. Only wider political support and engagement, especially at the level of the UNHCR Executive Committee and bilateral discussions

53

between China and interested governments, will lead to meaningful change in the Chinese position.

RI urges the United States government to make the status of North Korean refugees in China a priority issue in its on-going human rights dialogue with the Chinese government. We have raised this issue directly with officials of the State Department Bureaus of Population, Refugees, and Migration and Democracy, Human Rights, and Labor; they have assured us that this issue is indeed an important part of bilateral discussions with the Chinese. While RI accepts these assurances, we hope that the members of the Senate Committee on Foreign Relations and other members of the Senate will continue to impress upon the Administration the importance of Chinese action to facilitate UNHCR's access to North Korean refugees.

A second possible approach to protecting North Korean refugees is third country resettlement. Resettlement faces equally determined opposition from China. The Chinese authorities have actively tried to prevent North Koreans from reaching the embassies of potential resettlement countries and refuse to allow diplomatic missions to establish facilities to assess eligibility for resettlement in Yangbian itself. What little resettlement there has been has resulted from high-level defectors and other individuals reaching South Korea by boat or via underground railroad from China and the storming of embassy compounds in Beijing. The numbers are small. South Korea accepted fewer than 1,000 North Koreans for resettlement in 2002 even though their right to settle in the South is recognized in national law.

For resettlement to be a meaningful protection strategy, both China and South Korea will have to change their policies. China will have to allow potential resettlement countries open and unrestricted access to North Korean refugees. This step would be a logical follow on to a decision to allow UNHCR access to Yangbian, but neither action appears politically feasible at this point. As for South Korea, its low admission numbers reflect more than the difficulty of North Koreans reaching South Korea. As I learned on a visit to Seoul in June, South Korean citizens and the South Korean government have a remarkable ambivalence about the suffering of North Koreans. Citizens fear economic turmoil if North Koreans are admitted in large numbers, while their solidarity is limited by disdain for the poverty and lack of sophistication of North Koreans. As for the government, commitment to the Sunshine Policy and reconciliation more broadly locates the fundamental solution of humanitarian issues in gradual political change in North Korea that will result from engagement, rather than in large-scale acceptance of refugees, an act that would anger the leaders of the North Korean government. The result is a marked lack of commitment by South Korea to offer resettlement to North Koreans.

RI believes that in the near term resettlement is unlikely to be an option for more than a few thousand North Koreans. The U.S. role should be to engage with China to see if resettlement, at least on a modest scale, can become a legal option for North Koreans in China. The Administration should also be talking to the South Koreans about increasing their economic and political commitment to resettlement. The U.S. itself could be a resettlement destination. The U.S. experience with resettling previously isolated and difficult to assimilate populations, such as the Hmong from Laos, might be usefully applied to North Koreans, both by accepting them here and by providing technical training and support to South Korean government agencies and NGOs involved in resettlement. Finally, North Koreans, through the underground railway, have managed to reach countries as far away as Thailand and Cambodia. American embassy staff in Southeast Asian countries should be on the lookout for North Korean asylum seekers and be prepared to consider them for possible resettlement in U.S.

Senator BROWNBACK. Thank you all very much.

I regret to say we've got a vote that is on now, and so I'm going to have to proceed from here.

Let me say this, if I can, to each of you and to the panel before, I think this has been very illuminating. I'm regretful that it's taken this long to gather this much information. If I could, Mr. Hawk, from your testimony, that it strikes me this has been going on for some period of time and we're just now getting this little window on a very nasty place in the world. And it's just now come to the forefront.

Ms. Rios, let me thank you for what you're doing on this. Your grassroots movement has had a number of very successful efforts in trafficking in persons, dealing with that, and the Sudan, which we're hopeful getting close to a peace agreement near-term, Religious Freedom Act. I hope this is four in a row for you, that this one moves on forward, because this is clearly one of the worst situations we see in the world today, and ranks up there in the top category, historically, or at least over the last century.

Mr. Kumar, I appreciate your thoughts about the food aid. That is a wrestling issue that we're struggling with now, because a number of people assert that by giving food aid, it's being redirected toward the elite and the military and you're propping up the regime with food aid, even though the numbers I've seen, somewhere around a third of the North Korean population is being fed by international food donations, and perhaps even higher than that currently. So, obviously, it's—and we know that this is a very vulnerable population and nobody wants to hurt the people, but we also don't want to prop up a regime.

And Mr. Charny, I thought your points were excellent.

I, myself, have been to that region of the Chinese/North Korean border, just about a year ago. I wasn't as fortunate to interview people. They pretty well cleaned the place up, I guess, as you would say, before I got there, and everybody was told, "don't say anything." But the people I've interviewed that have come through the region pretty much correspond to what you've said, other than—I've heard a number of stories of people that if they've come out of North Korea into China and then taken back and found to have had contact with the underground railroad or religious people, that the detention can be much more severe, if not terminal, for them. Now, if it's a situation that you're basically trying to forage for food, that they're treated in a lighter fashion.

Mr. CHARNY. Can I just say, that's in my written testimony. But for obvious reasons, we weren't seeing people who had been either forced to admit or had been discovered being in contact with South Koreans or having converted to Christianity and agreeing to go back and proselytize. So our experience was limited to people who were fundamentally coming into China to survive, rather than ones who had been detained for these crimes, so-called, that are much more serious in nature from the North Korean standpoint.

Senator BROWNBACK. The trafficking issue, the trafficking in persons report, addresses some of that, as well, of women being trafficked out and, in essence, sold to groups of men to take care of homes, and sexually deal with the men as well, in the trafficking report.

So we're getting a lot of information from a number of different sources, all pointing to a cataclysmic human-rights situation in North Korea, and I think it's just absolutely imperative that we have this as part of the negotiations if we're going to negotiate with North Korea, and that the Chinese have to wake up to their responsibility in this area, that they've got to start to address this situation for the terrible situation that it is, or to start paying some sort of price, internationally, for continuing to ignore one of the worst human-rights abuses, if not the worst in the world today.

Thank you all very much for your work. I really do appreciate it, that of you and your organizations. Godspeed.

The hearing is adjourned.

[Whereupon, at 4:20 p.m., the subcommittee adjourned, to reconvene subject to the call of the Chair.]

ADDITIONAL STATEMENTS SUBMITTED FOR THE RECORD

STATEMENT SUBMITTED BY CITIZEN'S COALITION FOR HUMAN RIGHTS OF ABDUCTEES AND NORTH KOREAN REFUGEES

October 30, 2003

VIDEO STRIPS OF A NORTH KOREAN LABOR CAMP

We have photographic evidences of crimes committed against prisoners in a North Korean prison, including those forcibly repatriated defectors from China.

Ill-treatment of inmates in North Korean prison system has been common knowledge in the international community, yet there has been no solid evidence. Through underground contacts we obtained short video strips of North Korean Defector Labor Camps in Onsong district, North HamKyung Province. They were photographed in mid-August, 2003 and depict punishment of forcibly repatriated defectors from China, justifying refugee status for most of the current North Korean defectors in China, Russia, and south east Asian countries.

Normally, when North Korean defectors are apprehended in China, they are forcibly repatriated and are sent to work camps where they are forced into hard labor and subject to brutal torture. Until now, the international community has heard these stories while North Korean and Chinese authorities denied these accounts as fictitious or distorted stories.

By exposing these facts to the United States and to international society, we three South Korean NGOs urge all available means and resources be utilized in stopping the barbarous acts of the KIM, Jong-Il regime and the mechanisms of systematic oppression in North Korea be immediately dismantled. At the same time, we believe this is an opportune time to encourage Chinese authorities to officially recognize North Korean defectors as legitimate refugees as defined by international law.

Citizen's Coalition for the Human Rights of N.K Abductees and Refugees

Movement for the Dismantling of Camps for North Korean Political Prisoners

North Korean Network for Democratization

"The North Korea Freedom Coalition", where Citizen's Coalition for the Human Rights of N.K Abductees and Refugees is a member organization, is a bipartisan coalition of religious, human rights, non-governmental and Korean-American organizations, whose prime purpose is to bring freedom to the North Korean people and to ensure that the human rights component of U.S. and world policy towards North Korea receives priority attention.

CITIZEN'S COALITION FOR HUMAN RIGHTS OF ABDUCTEES AND NORTH KOREAN REFUGEES

November 3, 2003

PLEASE HELP TWO ARRESTED NORTH KOREAN WOMEN IN CHINA

Two North Korean women, Choi Sun-hwa, 56, and Song Jong-hwa, 23, mother and daughter, were among the unknown number of North Korean refugees who were arrested at the China/Vietnam border on 18 August 2003. There is no doubt that the above women will face severe punishment, if not execution, because they are former landlord's family, enemy of people. Attached is a testimony about their background. Please do not disclose the testimony at this stage. It was confirmed that they are still in China at the border prison of Tumen. Hopefully, the fact that they are still in China might be an indication of special consideration by the Chinese authorities. It is sincerely hoped that a little more push now will lead to their release as in the case of 7 North Korean defectors who were arrested in Shanghai with a Japanese aid worker some months ago and reportedly released later.

I would be very grateful if you and other supporters could urgently raise the issue with the Chinese authorities on their behalf. Your help for these two particular refugees would also apply to the other refugees in the same prison. Please help us! We believe your intervention works.

Many thanks as ever and kind regards,

SANG HUN KIM

PS: the attached testimony has a very brief reference to the death of an underground North Korean Christian. Will work hard to obtain further information and evidence, if possible, as soon as the other refugees from the same town are identified, both in China and Korea.

The following testimony was obtained in Seoul by an international human rights volunteer on 21 October, 2003.

ALAS! HAVE I SENT MY MOTHER AND SISTER TO HELL?

I am 28 years old (DOB: October, 1975). My name is Song Nip-sam, an alias. I was born in the Saetpyeol district of North Korea, one of the towns bordering China. My grandfather was a landlord and my father was socially discriminated for that reason. He had been a worker for life when he died from a stroke in 1996. I had a brother and two sisters. I joined the army in 1993 after I graduated from my hometown high school. I was so undernourished that I was discharged from the military service in 1994 after only a year of military service. I stayed home for about a year helping my mother with household affairs. I grew disillusioned and angry with the North Korean regime as we were socially discriminated against because of my family record.

I defected to China to seek freedom on 16 January 1997. On 6 December of the same year, I was grabbed by North Korean border guards on 6 December of the same year while attempting to return to North Korea to see my family. I was detained and interrogated by the State Security Agency (SSA) for a little over a month, after which I was cleared of all political offenses and released on 28 January 1998. During this time, however, I was kicked and beaten frequently. In the same cell of the SSA, I found a farmer by the name of Tokhung, a well-known figure in Hamyon of my home district, who was arrested 3 days before me. He earlier defected to China, sneaked into North Korea and was arrested while attempting to escape from China with his wife. He was severely beaten and badly tortured. He was still in the jail when I was released. About two months later after my release, every one in the town believed that he had been sent to a concentration camp and killed there, like the case of Mr. Kim Shi-wun, a factory inventory clerk and my fathers friend, about 50 at that time, was beaten to death by SSA for his record of defection to China in 1995. (I heard in China from somebody from my hometown that a woman oral hygiene doctor in my hometown was arrested for being a Christian by the Saepyeol District SSA sometime in 2000. She killed herself in jail by bumping her head hard against wall to refuse to tell other Christians' names under torture.)

My life in North Korea after my release was continuously under surveillance, and I was disappointed and angry with the North Korean regime and felt hopeless for my future. I defected to China for the second time on 10 March 1999, and finally managed to arrive alone in South Korea on 23 March 2001 via Mongolia. However, my happiness with freedom in South Korea was short-lived with thoughts of my mother and sister still in North Korea.

I managed to bring my mother, Choi Sun-hwa, 56, and sister, Song Jong-hwa, 23, to China on 12 June 2003. Alas, they were arrested by the Chinese authorities on 18 August while attempting to cross the Chinese border to Vietnam! I have no information about the circumstances under which they were arrested. There is no doubt that my mother and sister faced extremely harsh persecutions and punishment because of my grandfather's status. I am in such a state of agony that I would rather kill myself. The many sleepless nights I have now been through and the disappointment in not being able to turn to anyone for help makes me mad day and night and deprives me of laughter or any pleasure in life. I bitterly blame myself that I have sent them to hell! On this 22nd day of October 2003, I was able to confirm that they are still in a border prison in Tumen, China, which is surprising considering the usual speedy rate of repatriation to North Korea. Is it an indication of a change in the Chinese policy? Are my mother and sister going to be spared? May God help us.

○

www.ingramcontent.com/pod-product-compliance
Lightning Source LLC
Chambersburg PA
CBHW082152290526
45794CB00008B/3266

* 9 7 8 1 4 7 7 5 8 3 0 6 7 *